Public Finance in Underdeveloped Countries

Public Finance in Underdeveloped Countries

A. R. Prest MA, PhD

Professor of Economics
London School of Economics and Political Science

A HALSTED PRESS BOOK

JOHN WILEY & SONS
New York

© A. R. Prest 1962, 1972
Published in the U.S.A.
by Halsted Press, a Division
of John Wiley & Sons, Inc.
New York

Library of Congress Cataloging in Publication Data

Prest, Alan Richmond.
    Public finance in underdeveloped countries.

    "A Halsted Press book."
    Bibliography: p.
    1. Underdeveloped areas—Finance, Public.
I. Title.
HJ192.P68   1972   336'.09172'4   72-6436
ISBN 0-470-69697-4

Printed in Great Britain

Contents

Preface to the First Edition

This book is based on a series of seven lectures delivered at the Centro de Estudos de Estatistica Economica, Lisbon, in April 1961. The main body of the text is a revised and expanded version of the original lectures. The Appendices to the various chapters are reprints from previous work, apart from Chapter 6, Appendix II.

My first debt is to Professor C. Alves Martins, the Director of the Centro, and his colleagues who provided the original stimulus to write the lectures and gave me some valuable comments on them. Secondly, I have to thank Professor P. T. Bauer for many acute and penetrating comments. I also benefited greatly from the discussion of some of the chapters by the members of the Public Finance Workshop of Columbia University. Finally, I am indebted to the Department of Technical Co-operation, the Editors of the Economic Journal and Messrs Allen and Unwin for permission to reprint extracts from previous work.

Christ's College, Cambridge, 1962

A. R. Prest

Preface to the Second Edition

After an interval of ten years, it was necessary to make substantial changes. Chapters 1 to 3 resemble the first three chapters of the first edition outwardly, but their content has been updated and enlarged at many points (e.g. by incorporating the discussion of investment incentives previously in Chapter 4). On the other hand, deletions have also been made; for instance, the discussion of capital taxes has been taken out of Chapter 2 and now forms the nucleus of the new Chapter 4 on capital-based taxes. Chapter 5 is also new; this is an attempt to pull together some ideas which have been put forward for raising revenue, other than by the standard types of taxes. Chapter 6 is concerned with selected aspects of expenditure and Chapter 7 with legislative and administrative matters. Chapter 8 deals with regional financial issues. The Appendix relates to the particular problems of small countries, a subject which did not fit easily into the body of the text.

It will be observed that there are some major additions to and deletions from the topics covered in the first edition. Without listing them in detail it can be said that the main thrust of the changes has been to concentrate more exclusively than before on public finance in the narrower sense and not to attempt to cover such subjects as debt policy, foreign aid, development plan formulation and the like. The passage of time has also led to other changes; it seems a better use of space today not to devote a whole chapter to federal finances, but to discuss other regional financial issues as well. At the same time there are many resemblances between this edition and the previous one: the overall length is not very different, there is a heavier concentration on the revenue than on the expenditure side, the references tend to be biased towards Commonwealth countries and so on.

One always runs the risk of deceiving oneself with any *apologia pro editione secunda*; the real reason for change or non-change may be very prosaic indeed. But for what it is worth, we think that there are reasons of substance for choosing the particular course of action followed in this edition. It would have been easy to write a much expanded version; it takes a lot more time and effort to incorporate much new material and yet keep a book short. It would have been easy enough to reprint in their entirety various contributions to journals and conferences; but the coherence of the volume is (hopefully) greater when one confines oneself to drawing on such sources where relevant or enlightening. And in view of the avalanche of words dealing with wider problems of development, and the recent emergence of books on public finance taking the whole world as their stage, we also think that we can defend the degree of concentration to be found here.

In short, the first edition sprang from seven lectures given in 1961; it is hoped that the second edition will read as if it were based upon eight lectures given in 1971. It is not for one moment thought that it meets all conceivable needs in this field; for instance, we do not attempt to cover the important subject of tax-co-ordination between countries – nor do we pretend to be *au fait* with every recent fiscal development in every developing country. Our aim is simply to provide a general introduction to these matters, steering a middle course between superficial worldwide coverage and detailed country studies. The readership, or lack of it, must determine whether this is a sensible course or not.

Finally, thanks are due to a number of people who have helped with the preparation of material and of the manuscript. I must also acknowledge my great indebtedness to the Australian National University, Canberra. Appointment as a Visiting Professor for a period in 1971 provided the opportunity for concentrated work on the manuscript. Finally, I must express my gratitude for permission to reprint the Appendix.
London School of Economics, October 1971

A. R. Prest

1
Introduction

The title *Public Finance in Underdeveloped Countries* is open to many possible interpretations and so it would be as well to clarify our own at the very beginning. First of all, *Public Finance* can, at one extreme, be taken to cover the general subject of central government economic planning – a discussion of the merits and demerits of having a plan on the Indian model, for instance, or the most appropriate way of constructing such a policy framework. Another very different possibility would be to deal with purely descriptive matters – which sorts of taxes and expenditures one finds in developing countries, why the institutional arrangements differ, and so on. These two illustrations will be sufficient to show that it is quite impossible to cover all aspects of public finance in the course of a short survey and so we must be quite deliberately and openly selective.

Secondly, one must say something about the *underdeveloped countries* part of the title. Although a great deal of high grade mental effort has gone into defining the characteristics of such countries, one may wonder whether this is a very profitable activity. As Lord Morley is reputed to have said of elephants – he could not define one but nevertheless would have no trouble in recognising one. Similarly, we all know roughly what we mean by underdeveloped countries. They have certain features in common on the production side: one normally finds a high ratio of population to capital, a relatively high dependence on primary production of one sort or another and a relatively large subsistence element among these primary products. The detailed organisation of production may differ a great deal (compare the sugar estates of Barbados with the peasant cocoa farmers of Ghana), but the broad characteristics above continue to apply.

9

On the consumption side, the distinguishing feature is the low level of income and well-being compared to that found in the Western world.[1] Many of them also suffer from a marked short period instability of income and/or output.[2] Most underdeveloped countries are also characterised by rapidly growing populations. Whereas crude birth rates in European countries tend to be between 15 and 20 per thousand, one sometimes finds figures as high as 40–45 per thousand in Africa and Asia. Although crude death rates are understandably higher in underdeveloped countries, the net result is a much more rapid rate of growth of population, with figures of 3% p.a. or thereabouts being common and sometimes exceeded.[3]

As far as the rate of change of income per head is concerned, there is much less uniformity. On the one hand, it is possible to point to some countries where there has been an enormous development over the longer run (e.g. the growth in Nigerian exports – from some 65,000 tons of oilseeds p.a. in 1900 to about 1m tons p.a. in the early 1960s, quite apart from other products, especially the recent development of oil) and to others, where there has been a rapid rate of growth in more recent times (e.g. Jamaica and Kenya in the 1950s, South Korea and Taiwan in the 1960s). On the other hand, one can also find countries having a hard struggle to stay where they are without slipping backwards. Professor Meade's study of Mauritius[4] showed that real income per head fell by some 10% between 1953 and 1958. There are therefore very great differences

[1] In many African countries, for example, income per head is of the order of US $100–200 p.a., compared to the $2500, or so, common in N.W. Europe.

[2] E.g., a UN report (*International Compensation for Fluctuations in Commodity Trade*, New York, 1961) put the annual average fluctuation of export proceeds at some 9–12% in the post-war period. But see A. I. MacBean, *Export Instability and Economic Development* (Allen and Unwin, London, 1966) for many qualifications to the simple-minded ideas on this subject.

[3] Data from *United Nations Statistical Yearbook*, 1969 (UN, New York, 1970). It is perhaps worth noting that in this respect analogies with the development problem in Britain in the first half of the nineteenth century break down. In England and Wales, population only rose by 1.4% p.a., between 1811 and 1861.

[4] J. E. Meade *et al.*, *The Economic and Social Structure of Mauritius* (Methuen, London, 1961).

between these countries in this important – and, as some would say, supremely important – test of the rate of growth of income per head.

We may expect to find that these differences are often, though not invariably, correlated with differences between countries in respect of land endowment per head. It is much more likely that we shall find a slow rate of growth of income per head when the population is pressing heavily on the land area than when it is not. However, such major issues are not our prime concern here and we must resist the temptation to pursue them further now.

Rather, it would seem better to devote our remaining space in this chapter to the examination of two main questions. These can be phrased as follows: first, in what ways are public finance problems in developing countries found to differ from those elsewhere; and, second, it it important to distinguish public finance questions from the more general economic problems of developing countries? If the view were taken that public finance issues are identical whatever the general economic characteristics of a country, the case for selective treatment of developing countries would fail; similarly, if it were the case that public finance issues are trivial relatively to other economic problems in developing countries. In other words, the tests of difference and importance both have to be passed, to establish the case for a book specifically devoted to public finance in developing countries. It should be made clear here that the main emphasis at this stage will be on the positive rather than the normative aspects of these two major questions.

SPECIAL FEATURES OF THE PUBLIC FINANCES OF DEVELOPING COUNTRIES

We shall start by examining the differences between tax/income (or expenditure/income) ratios in developing and advanced countries and then look at the possible explanations of any such discrepancies. Subsequently, we shall have something to say about the differing composition of expenditure and revenue totals in the two sets of countries. Later, we shall look at the instability of revenue and expenditure over time.

Aggregate Ratios

The very first thing is to issue a warning about the many traps involved in compiling such data. Quite apart from all the practical problems of producing data on a more or less common basis, there are some decisions of principle to be taken. First, one has to decide whether primary interest is in the comparison between total expenditure or total revenue and a national aggregate: the first ratio will be more relevant to questions about the payments which the community has decided to make on a non-market basis whilst the other will be more concerned with the flow of purchasing power which is not at the direct disposal of the citizenry of a country.[1] Secondly, there are many decisions to be taken about the details of measurement and these in turn are interrelated with the objectives of measurement. To illustrate from the revenue side, there is the whole question of how far to include charges for services of a commercial type and, if the answer is something less than inclusion in full, how and where to draw the line between these charges and other forms of revenue. In fact, the best answer would seem to be inclusion of any excess profits element, but no more.[2] There are also plenty of difficulties in choosing an appropriate national aggregate e.g. gross or net, domestic or national, market price or factor cost concepts, and so on.[3]

It is not proposed to discuss these alternatives in detail here but simply to issue a warning that the data one finds in practice are most unlikely to satisfy all the relevant criteria, with the implication that we shall be extremely lucky if we can avoid biasses in comparisons between groups of developed and under-developed countries, let alone between individual countries.

[1] See A. R. Prest, 'Government Revenue, the National Income and all that' in R. M. Bird and J. Head (eds) *Modern Fiscal Issues* (Toronto University Press, Toronto, 1972); also C. S. Shoup, *Public Finance* (Weidenfeld and Nicolson, London, 1969), especially Chs. 3 and 20.

[2] *Ibid.*

[3] See, for instance, C. S. Shoup *et al.*, *The Tax System of Liberia* (Columbia University Press, New York, 1970), Ch. III.

12

Looking first of all at the revenue side, an examination of the figures given in the *UN Yearbook of National Accounts Statistics*[1] shows that the ratio of government revenue[2] to GDP at market prices over the latest three years available[3] was 18.5% for twenty-six developing countries and 31.2% for seventeen developed countries. Naturally, there is a wide dispersion round these mean figures (e.g. in the former group we find Zambia with more than 32% and the Philippines in the 10–11% range; and in the latter the Swedish figure is over 42%, more than double that of Portugal) but nevertheless the difference would seem to be significant, both statistically and economically.[4] On the expenditure side, we find a much smaller difference between the ratios of government consumption expenditure to GNP (12.3% in developing countries; 14.8% in developed). The main explanation of the contrast between the revenue and expenditure data is to be found in the much greater relative importance of transfer payments in the more advanced countries.

There are various possible explanations of these differences. One is that there may be fewer pressures on governments in developing countries to incur public expenditure; alternatively, it may be that the constraint is to be found on the revenue side, either in terms of lack of revenue-raising capacity or in unwillingness to make the necessary efforts to raise taxes. We must obviously spend some time appraising each of these possible explanations.

Spending Pressures

In analysing spending pressures in developing countries, we can start by looking at the movements of recorded expenditure, or revenue, relatively to GNP over time. There is plenty of evidence

[1] UN, New York, 1970.
[2] Usually central government revenue only.
[3] Usually 1966, 1967 and 1968.
[4] It should be noted that when such data are studied in detail there is not much evidence that the revenue/GNP ratio is a simple function of income per head within any given income range. The big differences are to be found in the ratios at the opposite ends of the income spectrum (*cf.* R. A. Musgrave, *Fiscal Systems* (Yale University Press, New Haven, 1969), p. 111).

to show that there have been sharp upward movements in such data over the post-war period.[1] But all we can show by parading figures of this sort is what was *actually* spent by governments. This is some guide, but in the nature of things only a partial guide, to the long term *pressure* on governments to spend. There is clearly no way of translating this latter notion into a hard and fast set of figures but at the same time we must make an attempt to appraise the intensity of such pressures and the reasons for them.

There seem to be three main reasons contributing to strong pressures to spend (leaving aside general price changes): the growth of population, the emergence of strong local opinions and the emergence of strong world opinions. Let us look at each of these in turn.

We have already sketched in the general population picture in these countries and so we can proceed straight to the financial implications. A rapid rate of growth of population will have obvious repercussions on the needs for roads, public housing, sewers and water supply etc. And any given rate of total growth will imply a more than proportionate rate of growth of the number of children and, therefore, a more than proportionate need to expand educational facilities. Rapid increases in populations are frequently associated with movements from rural to urban areas;[2] as standards of public services tend to be higher in the latter, this is likely to mean a more than proportionate increase in government outlay. Although it is not necessary for all types of government expenditure (e.g. central administration) to increase at the same rate as population grows, the opportunities for productivity increases are likely to be small in many branches of government (e.g. teachers, policemen). So the

[1] E.g. A. Maddison, *Economic Progress and Policy in Developing Countries* (Allen and Unwin, London, 1970), p. 71, shows that the domestic revenue/GNP ratio rose from an average of 15% in 1950 to 20% in 1965 for twenty developing countries. See also R. J. Chelliah, 'Trends in Taxation in Developing Countries', *International Monetary Fund Staff Papers*, July, 1971, for detailed information on a large number of countries.

[2] *Cf.* U. K. Hicks, *Development from Below* (Oxford University Press, Oxford, 1961), p. 233.

likelihood is that the rate of growth of government expenditure as a whole is likely to be faster than that of population.[1]

But even growth rates of 3 % p.a. of population by no means fully explain the great increases of government expenditure which have taken place in many countries. So we must now look at the second of our three reasons – the emergence of strong local opinions. There are several strands, some economic and some non-economic, to this argument. First, there is the world-wide demand for improvements in living standards. Social services of all kinds – housing provision, social security benefits, hospitals and so on – are in acute demand throughout the whole world. Nor is the clamour less for expenditure which may be expected to yield additional income in the longer run (education, public works etc.).

There is a further point to notice in this connection. Provision of some goods and services may be a much more onerous undertaking in some of these countries than one might think at first sight. Suppose we take the case of hospitals. It is not unknown to have cyclones and hurricanes in tropical countries and it is no use having a hospital which blows down when the houses are blown down by the hurricane: this is the very time it is needed. Consequently, one must cater for hurricane-proof hospitals, with all the attendant financial consequences. Similarly, the achievement of any given education standard is just that much more expensive when dealing with a multi-racial society with a multiplicity of languages and traditions. An excellent case can be made without the slightest trouble for each line of expenditure considered by itself – social security is a 'must' for a self-respecting society, road improvements are indispensable, modern sanitation is urgent and so on – but that is a very different matter from saying that they can all be pursued at once.

We could obviously spend a lot of time trying to analyse why there has been this sudden awakening to the possibilities of economic and social improvement. The events of wartime and

[1] See Chapter 7 for discussion of productivity growth rates in the public sector relatively to the private sector and the implications for the ratio of taxation to GNP.

the enforced contacts between people with high and people with low standards of living had something to do with it. The post-war development of air transport and the consequent greater ease of communication between rich and poor countries, between temperate and tropical peoples, has made contacts easier still. Allied to this development is an increasing belief that countries can do something to improve their own economic destiny and that they are not entirely at the mercy of blind economic forces. That this is a recent change can be seen from the fact that Development Plans were unknown in British colonial territories before the Second World War (we need not debate at this stage whether Development Plans are synonymous with growth and development, but simply take them as an indication that a lot of people are now alive to the possibilities of economic progress). Perhaps most important of all have been the immense political changes of the last two decades. Did anyone foresee in, say, 1950 the number of independent members of the United Nations in 1970? If he had openly quoted the present figure, he would in all probability have been laughed at.

Fascinating as this historical probing is, it does take us far outside the realms of analytical economics and so we must leave it and return to our main theme. The awakening to the desirability and possibility of economic improvement has been accompanied by a growth in the belief that it is the duty of Government to purchase many goods and services (especially capital goods), to produce some of them itself and to take some steps to redistribute income between different sections of the community. It is not part of our task to ask whether this is good or bad; it is simply presented as a fact. Evidence is plentiful. The preparation of national Development Plans by governments is one general indication; and in so far as a predominant role is assigned to the public sector in the plan (e.g. in respect of capital formation in India) the lesson is clearer still. The common jargon of the age – e.g. resource mobilisation or the public provision of infrastructure – is another. Suffice it to say that the change compared to pre-1939, when a government was thought of as the organisation which simply held the ring within which economic activity was carried on by companies and business men, is startlingly great. The very minimum that a government is expected to do nowadays in any country is to remove or cut down the obstacles to economic grow thmet by the private sector and, much more frequently, it is deemed to have the task of striving for growth in a positive manner both by example and by precept.

The reasons for this popular attitude – some might say faith – are many. Once again, the influence of the wartime role of governments must be remembered. This should not be over-estimated, however. The UK was, perhaps, the country which mobilised itself for war more fully than any other and this left many marks on the economy. But by and large the tide of government control receded in the postwar period to such an extent that the degree of general intervention in the economy today is obviously less than in many of the underdeveloped countries, even if we exclude the Soviet countries. There can be no question that this belief in government action has been fostered in some countries by apathy and stagnation among local business communities.[1] This has reinforced the notion that governments *should* undertake various responsibilities by the further notion that government is the only organisation which *can* undertake them.

Whatever the reasons, and in no way are we trying to go into them fully, the plain fact is that it is now not only accepted but expected that government should take strong positive action to foster development. This brings us to another point. Not only does the population at large expect government action; it also has the power to enforce it, through the medium of the ballot box. Constitutional developments have given the keys of power in most countries to the population at large. Whereas before the Second World War government was in the hands of Europeans and indigenous members of the population played no part at all in it, we are now in a position where the reverse holds. There can be many different views about the most desirable rate of

[1] A revealing picture of the problems of a small isolated territory is to be found in J. W. F. Rowe, *The Economy of the Seychelles and its Future Development* (mimeographed, September 1958).

17

political change, but no one can challenge the fact that political power in most of the countries we are discussing rests fairly and squarely on the shoulders of the local politicians today. This may have some consequences which we deplore and which may not even be in the best interests of the countries concerned, e.g. the election into office of demagogues who offer the earth to the voters, but such points are not our concern as economists.[1] The simple fact is that the inhabitants of most of these countries now have the power to choose the government they want and throw out the government they do not want.[2]

We have traced out the implications of the emergence of strong local opinions: the belief in positive action to raise living standards, the view that any government should be a principal in such action and the power to reject a government which does not promise to play such a part. It is time to turn to the remaining reason for the pressure on government spending: the emergence of strong world opinions.

There is clearly no hard and fast line between the consequences of local and world opinions. No one can say for certain how far the growth of, say, education or health expenditures in any given country is due to a government's desire to placate local opinion or to its wish to conform with or emulate practices in other countries. But there can be no doubt that the emergence of world interest in these matters has made for greater pressure on governments to increase their level of spending.

World interest focuses itself in a number of ways - United Nations debates, economists' conferences, International Agency missions and so on. Indeed, it could be argued that interdependence of choice ('the demonstration effect') is more important

[1] Except in the not infrequent cases when the earth is delivered in the form of jobs in government service, with consequential boosting of government expenditures.

[2] It might be said that in a number of newly independent countries democratic voting procedures have not been very successful, with the consequent rise to power of military or para-military regimes. This is no doubt true. But most of the evidence seems to be that such regimes indulge in relatively more government economic activity than one finds in the more democratic countries. This should not surprise us; there is after all a pre-supposition that most military minds will work in this way.

for public than for personal expenditures. If any one feels that it can be argued that such spotlighting of underdeveloped countries enables government expenditure to be reduced, it is reasonable to ask him to produce his evidence. *Prima facie* one would feel that precisely the opposite is the case.

We can therefore conclude that for these various reasons – population growth, local opinions, world opinions – developing countries are under extremely strong pressures to expand the size of the public sector. Indeed, the results of such pressures are very clearly reflected in the budgetary history of Ceylon, India and Pakistan in the 1960s.[1] The excess of current and capital expenditure over current revenue increased in absolute terms in all three countries, so that towards the end of the decade it was at least twice the figure prevailing at the beginning, and in Ceylon the percentage ratio of the deficit to the total of revenue collected also increased.[2] These cases may not be fully representative but at least they do suggest that in three Asian countries there was no evidence of any absence of spending pressures. It is surely highly implausible that deficits would have increased so much if the explanation of smaller tax/income ratios than in more developed countries were to be found on the expenditure rather than the revenue side. Accordingly, we must now ask whether constraints of taxable capacity or tax effort are more convincing explanations.

Taxable Capacity and Tax Effort
It is now well recognised that the notion of taxable capacity means very little in any absolute sense. One relevant determinant is whether revenue is being raised for making transfer payments or for public absorption of goods and services. Another is the composition of the latter – willingness to pay taxes may differ markedly, if expenditure is on defence rather than education provision. And it goes without saying that the concept of

[1] C. T. Edwards, 'Financing Government Spending: Ceylon, India, Pakistan', *Economic Bulletin for Asia and the Far East* (UN, Bangkok), December 1969.

[2] E.g. for 1955/6–1959/60 (average) the deficit, as defined above, was Rs. 241m, and in 1968/9 (est.) it was Rs. 928m; whereas total revenue had risen from some Rs. 1100m, to some Rs. 2000m, over this period.

'subsistence' is so vague that we make no progress by postulating that government can in some sense skim off productive resources so that people are reduced to that level but no further.[1]

Recent econometric studies[2] do enable us to make some progress, however. The technique which has been evolved is to assess the main influences (e.g. income level, openness, degree of administrative capacity, etc.), making for differences in tax/ GNP ratios between countries and then compare actual ratios achieved with those predicted on the basis of the regression equation.

With appropriate specification the sizes of the residuals can be taken as a measure of tax effort, on the grounds that differences in taxable capacity (including those due to the greater availability as development proceeds of 'tax handles,' to use Musgrave's vivid phrase) will be taken care of by the explanatory variables in the regression equations. To illustrate from one such exercise relating to forty-nine developing countries[3] an explanation of tax/income ratios was conducted in terms of the relative importance of the agricultural and the mining (including oil) shares of income. The former was selected as being closely related to the stage of development; and the latter as indicative of the structure of an economy and also as preferable to a simple indicator of openness, such as the share of exports in GNP.

As might be expected the coefficient of the agricultural share variable was negative and that of the mining share variable positive ($\bar{R}^2 = .411$). Although there was some slight evidence that countries with less taxable capacity made higher tax efforts,[4] there was no really systematic relationship. Countries could in

---

[1] *Cf.* A. R. Prest, *op. cit.*, for fuller discussion.

[2] There is now a large number of studies on these lines. The most relevant for our purposes are J. R. Lotz and E. R. Morss, 'Measuring Tax Effort in Developing Countries', *IMF Staff Papers*, November 1967; R. A. Musgrave, *Fiscal Systems* (Yale University Press, New Haven, 1969); and R. W. Bahl, 'A Regression Approach to Tax Effort & Tax Ratio Analysis', *IMF Staff Papers*, November 1971.

[3] Bahl, *op. cit.*

[4] The relative positions of Ceylon and Malaysia also illustrate this proposition. Ceylon has a higher ratio of tax revenue to GNP despite disadvantages in respect

fact be divided quite neatly into four groups – high capacity and high effort (e.g. Zambia), high capacity and low effort (e.g. Trinidad), low capacity and high effort (e.g. Sudan) and low capacity and low effort (Pakistan). So this analysis would suggest that either low taxable capacity or low effort[1] or a mixture of both will explain why many developing countries exhibit smaller ratios of tax yield to GNP than those found in Western Europe or North America. In other words, the revenue constraint, whether in one guise or the other, appears to be a much more likely explanation than the suggestion that spending pressures on the public sector are so much less in developing countries.

Needless to say, there are plenty of question marks attached to these econometric studies. The very fact that results differ quite markedly depending on the period studied, the precise specification of the regression equation, the sample of countries and so on is sufficient evidence of that.[2] And it must be emphasised that the results have no normative significance: there is no necessary implication that a country which appears to be making a low tax effort should necessarily make a higher one. It could simply be that all the other countries in the sample are 'wrong', and it is 'right'.

of openness and income per head. The explanations seem to be a more interventionist philosophy and the tax structure itself (*cf.* C. T. Edwards, *Public Finances in Malaya and Singapore*, Australian National University Press, Canberra, 1970), p. 53.

[1] It should be understood that the concept of low effort embraces both the case where the number of taxes or rates of tax are low and that where the main failure is on the collection side.

[2] R. A. Musgrave, *Fiscal Systems*, *op. cit.*, p. 124: 'The evidence remains puzzling and in need of further explanation, including greater emphasis on what we have called the non-economic factors.' But it should be noted that R. W. Bahl, 'A Representative Tax System Approach to Measuring Tax Effort in Developing Countries' (to be published) shows that much the same rankings of countries by tax effort and tax capacity can be obtained by a different approach, i.e. one where *tax effort* is defined as actual tax yield ÷ yield of representative tax system (the denominator being estimated by relating the average of the effective tax rates for the whole sample of countries to the relevant base for an individual country) and *tax capacity* is the ratio of the estimated yield of the representative tax system to GNP in a country.

To recapitulate, we have found that tax revenue/income ratios differ significantly between developing and developed countries. Furthermore, the lower figures prevailing in developing countries are not to be explained in terms of lack of pressure for public spending but rather by constraints of taxable capacity and tax effort. So whereas it is sometimes argued that the expenditure side plays the leading role in more advanced countries, this would not appear to be so in developing areas. It is also unwise to assume that increments of revenue can be analysed on their own; spending pressures are likely to be such that additional revenue will often be accompanied by spending increases rather than by an increased budget surplus.[1]

Expenditure Composition

For a number of countries, we now have a common form of classification of government expenditure provided by the UN. If we group more developed and less developed countries separately, we then have the following results.

TABLE 1
Percentages of Central Government Expenditure (1967–9 average)

	Underdeveloped Countries	Developed Countries
Economic Classification		
Current goods and services	50.1	34.9
Gross domestic capital formation	17.4	10.3
Current transfers	22.5	41.0
of which debt interest	5.5	5.6
Functional Classification		
Education	17.7	12.8
Defence	11.3	14.1

Source: *UN Statistical Yearbook* 1969 (UN, New York, 1970)

[1] *Cf.* S. Please, 'Mobilising Internal Resources Through Taxation' in R. E. Robinson (ed.), *Developing The Third World: Experience of the 1960s* (Cambridge University Press, Cambridge, 1971).

Notes: 1. Underdeveloped is unweighted average of Ceylon, Chile, Dominican Republic, Ecuador, El Salvador, Ethiopia, Ghana, Honduras, India, Liberia, Kenya, Korea, Malaysia, Malawi, Mexico, Nigeria, Peru, Philippines, Southern Rhodesia, Thailand, Tanzania, Togoland, Zambia.

2. Developed is unweighted average of Australia, Austria, Belgium, Canada, Denmark, Finland, France, West Germany, Ireland, Israel, Italy, Japan, Netherlands, New Zealand, Norway, Portugal, Sweden, UK.

3. Figures usually refer to central government only; but lower tiers are included in a few cases.

4. There are small differences of definition in the various items and in some cases the years covered differed slightly from 1967–9.

It goes without saying that, despite the great efforts made to ensure consistency between definitions and classification, there must inevitably be some elements of noncomparability here. It also goes without saying that there are large variations around the mean figures shown in the table. Despite these reservations, it does seem fair to say that there are some major differences between the two columns of figures. First, the importance of current goods and services relatively to transfer payments is clearly greater in the underdeveloped group. This is what one would expect *a priori*. For even though defence expenditure (countries like Korea apart) tends to be of less importance in the underdeveloped group, the combination of large expenditures on health and education and the embryonic state of many social security systems might be expected to predominate and so produce the result we see in the Table. We do not propose to analyse the reasons for these differences in detail at this stage but it might be noted that education expenditure can be championed as part of capital formation; and the comparative lack of social security arrangements is not such a glaring gap when one has extensive systems of aid by kinsfolk, members of the same tribe, etc.

Another striking feature of Table 1 is the relatively greater importance in developing countries of gross fixed capital formation. This is very clear evidence of the way in which the pressure for economic advance has pushed or pulled governments into a major role in the working of the economy.

A number of attempts have been made in recent years to derive econometric explanations of expenditure components.[1] So far they have not proved very satisfactory; and the results from time series data have differed quite considerably from those from cross-section analysis. No doubt improvements will be recorded in such exercises in time but in the meanwhile two further observations can be made. One is that the applicability of the concept of income elasticity of demand in this context needs to be questioned. Although such notions clearly play their part (e.g. people do seem to want expenditure on education and health to rise proportionately faster than income), it seems doubtful whether they take one far enough in these matters. Quite apart from the need to bring in additional economic notions (e.g. how far are demands for educational expenditure consequential on changes in tastes as well as changes in income) there is the fundamental point that we have a political process of choice as well as an economic process at work. Even though one may not wish to go as far as accepting the so-called 'law of ever-increasing state activity', propounded by the German economist Wagner in the last century, one can still agree that abstract economic reasoning of the standard kind cannot do more than provide part of the answer. Finally, it is a commonplace of fiscal theory today to argue that, in certain circumstances, an incremental pound of government spending on goods and services will tend to have greater income generating effects than an incremental pound of government spending on transfer payments. Correspondingly, it can be argued that if the marginal pound of transfer payments is accompanied by a marginal pound of revenue, there will, as a first approximation, be no effects on the level of income; whereas if the extra revenue is

[1] See R. A. Musgrave, *Fiscal Systems*, *op. cit.*, Chs. 3 and 4.

accompanied by extra spending on goods and services there will be some income generating effects. If marginal transactions follow the same pattern as those shown in Table 1 we should expect that in underdeveloped countries the marginal pound of spending accompanying the marginal pound of revenue will have a greater goods content and a smaller transfer content than in developed countries. We might expect that on this account the income generating effects of extra spending financed through extra taxation would be greater in the underdeveloped parts of the world – though relatively greater import leakages, not least due to the importance of capital formation in government spending, will work in the other direction.

Revenue Composition
Developing countries differ from more advanced countries in revenue composition in some fairly well-known ways. First, the relative importance of consumption-based taxes is greater in the former – customarily providing some 70–80% of total tax revenue rather than 40–50%. The mining and oil countries do not fit into this generalisation, but the phenomenon is widespread all the same. Export taxes play important roles in some developing countries (e.g. more than 20% of total revenue in Ghana) whereas they are virtually unknown in the more developed parts of the world. And import duties customarily account for a much larger fraction of the total. As for the remaining sources of revenue, corporation taxes are less prominent in many countries for reasons we shall explore in due course, and although capital taxes in one form or another are ubiquitous in more developed countries, this is not so in tropical Africa for instance. This subject will be explored further in Chapter 4. Finally, foreign aid often plays an important part in public sector financing. Econometric investigations into the determinants of the yield from different taxes in different countries have been numerous.[1] A fair judgment seems to be that so far it has not proved possible to isolate simple explanations; in particular, what may seem to be a promising approach

[1] See e.g. Musgrave, *ibid*, p. 142 ff.

25

for all countries taken together often breaks down when one takes sub-groups of poorer or richer countries. At the same time there would appear to be less conflict between results from historical and cross-section approaches than in expenditure components analysis.

Revenue and Expenditure Instability

Fluctuations in export prices and quanta are common in developing countries. These fluctuations may be due to changes on the supply side or the demand side, or a mixture of the two. Examples of instability due to the supply side are easy to find in the last few years with hurricanes in the Caribbean, tidal waves in East Pakistan and so on. Less dramatic but no less serious in their effects are the periodic losses of crops due to locusts, drought or excessive rains which so often occur with tropical agriculture. On the demand side, there are two reasons for violent fluctuations; first, exports are frequently a high proportion of GNP,[1] (or at least of the cash component of GNP) and secondly one or two commodities often bulk large in exports. Therefore, changes in demand conditions for one or two commodities may be sufficient to generate large changes in incomes. Examples of the first reason are Barbados with exports running at more than 50% of GNP and to illustrate the second we can take Mauritius as an estate economy (95% of exports from sugar) Ghana as a peasant economy (50–60% of exports from cocoa) and Zambia as a mining economy.

It can, of course, be argued that any country, developed, half-developed or underdeveloped, can suffer natural disasters. It can also be argued that there is just as much chance that a shortfall on the demand side will coincide with a shortfall as with a surplus on the supply side. So one must be careful not to get these matters out of perspective. Nevertheless, the fact remains that the public finances of underdeveloped countries are liable to suffer severe short term embarrassments. These may take the form of reductions in the proceeds of taxes levied on the profits of exporters, or taxes on the exports themselves,

[1] Though not always; India is an important exception, for instance.

and in so far as smaller exports lead to a reduction of imports, this may also cut government revenue severely if it is heavily dependent, as so often is the case, on import duties.

To illustrate, it has been recorded that Malayan revenue is liable to suffer from the fact that rubber and tin prices tend to move in the same direction – it is very rare for one price to rise and for the other to fall.[1] Similarly, there are many recorded instances of falls in world metal prices leading to much more than proportionate changes in tax yield payable by companies operating in developing countries e.g. the fall in the world price of copper from around £350 a ton in 1956 to around £200 a ton in 1958 led to a much more than proportionate reduction in the yield of income tax from the copper companies in Northern Rhodesia (as Zambia then was).[2]

In order to get such changes into perspective, we need only ask what effects would follow in the UK if the yield of a main tax – say, income tax – fell by a quarter between one year and the next due to circumstances outside the control of the UK government. Deficit finance on this scale has more often been preached than practised in developed economies; in the under-developed, the tendency is the other way round.

Nor is it just a matter of revenue fluctuations. In so far as the goods and services component of government expenditure is a larger percentage of the total than in developed countries (see page 22) the possibilities of curtailing expenditure in years of revenue shortfall may well be fewer. This does not necessarily follow: some goods and services expenditure can be cut at short notice and some grants and transfers cannot (and, indeed, may rise rather than fall in the case of unemployment benefits). But it seems a reasonable generalisation.

Some final comments may be in order on these differences in the character of the public finances of developing economies. To

---

[1] *Cf.* C. T. Edwards *Public Finances in Malaya and Singapore* (Australian National University Press, Canberra, 1970) p. 86.
[2] Net operating profits of all companies fell from £78m. to £26m. in this period.

meet the long run growth of government expenditure, it is desirable that the tax system as a whole should be income-elastic in character.[1] In so far as governments are expected to finance not only their own expenditure but also to budget for a sufficient excess of revenue over expenditure to enable private investment to take place without inflationary consequences, this may be so *a fortiori* depending on the relative rate of growth of public spending on the one hand and private investment (relatively to private saving) on the other. This could mean either or both of two things: that each individual tax should be so arranged that its yield is elastic with respect to national income changes (e.g. a progressive income tax rather than a poll tax), or that those taxes whose yield is highly elastic with respect to national income should be predominant in the revenue structure.

If the tax system can be set up like this, dangers of perpetual budgetary imbalance will be much less. But if the tax structure is arranged in this way, we immediately run up against the fact that the yield is likely to be elastic with respect to short-run fluctuations in national income as well as to the long term trend. (This need not be the case if there were very different changes in the distribution of income in the two cases, but that would be an entirely fortuitous result.) It might be thought at first sight that this is highly desirable; it is now orthodox doctrine that a government should run a deficit when there is a short-term downswing in incomes in the private sector. However, such a policy is not at all plain sailing in many underdeveloped countries, as there frequently are situations where deficit financing is inappropriate. First, the reason for long-term persistence of unemployment or under-employment is much more likely to be a lack of co-operating factors of production – capital, technical knowledge, skilled foremen and so on – rather than a deficiency of aggregate demand. Secondly, the likely causes of short-term fluctuations in incomes are reductions in the demand for exports, crop failures, etc., rather than downswings in the level of

[1] For estimates of income elasticity of tax yields in India see G. S. Sahota *Indian Tax Structure and Economic Development* (Asia Publishing House, Bombay, 1961); also M. M. Jain, *Economic and Political Weekly*, 3 May 1969.

domestic investment. In neither of these cases can a government deficit be financed by internal borrowing without running risks of generating inflationary pressures or balance of payments disequilibria or both.

Another point is the clash between the requirements of a long run sensitivity of tax receipts to income and the requirements of the incentives to work, to save and to take risks. We shall develop this point further as we proceed, but we can say here and now that if, for instance, we lay especially heavy indirect taxes on durable consumer goods (on the grounds that, income elasticity of demand for such goods being high, tax yield will tend to rise more than proportionately to income), we may be loading our taxes on to just those goods which people would wish to buy out of marginal earnings if they did, in fact, work fractionally harder. This is a dilemma common to any tax system in any country but it may well be a particularly serious one for the fiscal systems of the countries which interest us here. It may also be the case that many developing countries are less concerned with income redistribution via the fiscal process. To this extent support for progressive taxes and a high elasticity of tax receipts to income is weakened.

THE IMPORTANCE OF FISCAL METHODS IN DEVELOPING COUNTRIES

So far we have been looking at major differences between the public finances of developing and developed countries. We must now turn to our other leading question: is the subject matter of public finance important in the context of the economics of development? We shall not need to spend as long on this topic as on the previous one but nevertheless it is imperative to see what answer should be given to this question.

There would seem to be two sorts of cases in which one could dismiss public finance questions as being trivial in developing economics. The first would be where one has a very small degree of public intervention; the second would be where, despite extensive public intervention, reliance on fiscal as distinct from other instruments is at a minimum. Let us examine each of these two possibilities in turn.

At first it might seem that there is a case for saying that developing countries are characterised by small public sectors; as we saw earlier (page 13), the tax/GNP or expenditure/GNP ratios are usually smaller than in more developed countries. But there is a great difference between this proposition and any suggestion that the public sector is of no importance in developing countries. For one thing, the overall tax/GNP or expenditure/GNP ratio is only a partial measure of the importance and power of the public sector e.g. a small amount of revenue from a commodity tax may mean that it is doing its job very effectively in the sense of discouraging output and/or consumption of that item. Furthermore, there has been a significant increase in these ratios over the last few years and it is a major policy objective in many countries to increase them further. Finally, such ratios tell us very little about the degree of public intervention in a wider sense e.g. the importance of government-owned utilities, airlines, shipping lines, banks, insurance companies and the like. Any survey of such elements of government activity[1] is sufficient to dispel any suspicion of a thought that public sector activity is an unimportant ingredient in the economies of such countries.

We still have another hurdle to surmount – the proposition that even though one may have a large amount of government intervention in some general sense, fiscal policies and methods are unimportant. This clearly could be so. One might have a large area of publicly organised production but such goods and services could nevertheless be sold on the market exactly like those which are privately produced. Alternatively, even though a government might hope to divert an economy from the courses which it would otherwise take, its main instruments could be monetary or physical controls rather than fiscal ones.

[1] A. H. Gantt II and G. Dutto 'Financial Performance of Government-Owned Corporations in the less Developed Countries', *IMF Staff Papers*, March 1968.

Thus it is sometimes argued that fiscal instruments are relatively unimportant in the highly planned economy of Soviet Russia; and that the relative longevity of Soviet finance ministers in office is circumstantial evidence of their unimportance.

Whether such propositions carry much conviction in relation to the countries concerning us here is very much more doubtful. There are literally hundreds of ways[1] in which they rely on tax or expenditure policies for achieving their objectives e.g. tax concessions to encourage foreign investors, budgetary surpluses to increase total savings and so on. We do not imply that tax policy is important in every context e.g. its role may well be more limited in smoothing out fluctuations in real or money incomes in highly open than in more closed economies; and administrative limitations may circumscribe its usefulness in the correction of the harmful effects of externalities. Nor are we at this stage concerned with the optimal role of fiscal policy relatively to other instruments of intervention. All we are concerned to argue – and to argue forcibly – is that the usual public finance instruments are of unquestionable importance in many developing countries. Indeed, when the god worshipped in many of them is faster growth it could hardly be otherwise; for if the engine of growth is the public sector, one is likely to need a lot of revenue; whereas if it is primarily the private sector one is likely to need a lot of incentives or at least an absence of disincentives, and so we are inextricably involved in public finance measures in either case. The same conclusion can be reached from another angle; administrative inexperience is likely to be even more of a drawback in imposing direct controls than taxes; and most of these countries have a much longer tradition of running tax systems than monetary policies – indeed many of them have only had Central Banks for a few years.

CONCLUSION

In the light of these arguments, we can conclude that both the questions which were posed initially can be answered in the

[1] Even if they are not always made very explicit; e.g. many Development Plans have relatively little to say about tax structures and tax roles.

31

affirmative. There are features of the public finances of developing countries which differentiate them from other countries; and public finance is a non-negligible instrument of policy in developing countries.

2

Income-based Taxes

In this chapter we shall examine the possibilities and likely consequences of meeting the heavy and increasing programmes of government spending by taxes based on income. We shall not attempt any refined definition of what should or should not be classed under this heading but will confine ourselves to personal and company income taxation.[1]

Before coming to individual taxes, it may be useful to look at the general pattern of taxation in a number of countries. Examination of forty-one countries covered by UN data[2] showed that the relative importance of taxes on income and wealth, as a proportion of central government revenue, was markedly less in the developing countries. For twenty-three such countries the unweighted average ratio was 21.6 % (maximum Mexico 44.9 %; minimum Togo 9.7 %) whereas for eighteen advanced countries the corresponding figure was 34.2 % (maximum New Zealand 60.2 %; minimum Norway 19.9 %). Needless to say, there are plenty of snags in such calculations (e.g. the data relate to income and wealth taxes taken together; the USA percentage is ostensibly very much greater than that of the UK, but this is because the USA figure relates only to the federal government and so excludes the state governments) but the broad pattern which emerges is indisputably clear: that income-based taxes make a much smaller contribution to total revenue in developing than in developed countries. The position is changing over time[3] but

---

[1] Expenditure or spendings tax is dealt with in Chapter 3 on the grounds that it has more affinity to consumption-based than to income-based taxes; capital taxes are all grouped together in Chapter 4; and payroll taxes are considered together with social security taxes in Chapter 5.

[2] *UN Statistical Yearbook*, 1969 (UN, New York, 1970).

[3] For evidence about the changes in the Latin American position in the 1960s see R. M. Bird and O. Oldman, 'Tax Research and Tax Reform in Latin America', *Latin American Research Review*, Vol. III, No. 3, Summer 1968.

nevertheless the general truth of the proposition is likely to hold for many years to come.

PERSONAL INCOME TAXATION

In the case of personal income taxation, there is a very great deal of difference between the two types of countries. We can see this in a number of different ways. In the UK some 20 million individuals pay income tax each year and in the USA some 65 million – i.e. of the order of 30–40% of the *total* (not just the adult) population of the country. In many underdeveloped countries, on the other hand, it is a real achievement to reach a figure of 5%.[1] Whereas income assessed to personal income tax amounts to some 70% of GNP in the UK, we find figures of 22% in Jamaica and 24% in Fiji and a good deal less than that in many other countries.

As always, there can be plenty of argument about the comparability of the data. But differences of this magnitude are clearly not going to be explained away by imperfections in the statistics; they must represent fundamental differences in the coverage and operation of income taxation. It would seem that there are four reasons for the radically different performance of personal income tax in underdeveloped countries. First, there are problems of defining income. Second, there are difficulties of assessing any one individual's income, even if one knows how to define income in general. Third, there are matters connected with the fixing of rates and allowances. Fourth, there are problems of assessment. Let us examine each of these in turn and in some detail.

The definition of income in an advanced country gives rise to all sorts of conundra which can hardly be said to have been solved to everyone's satisfaction. To take one of the most obvious difficulties: ought capital gains to be regarded as part of

[1] E.g. in 1964, the figure for Malaysia was 4% and that for Singapore 6% of the *adult* population (*cf.* C. T. Edwards, *op. cit.*, p. 88), but these figures are much higher than those found in typical African countries or in the Indian subcontinent.

34

personal income or not? By and large, the British answer until recently has been 'No' and the American 'Yes'. It must be said straightaway that this is an over-simplification of the tax law of the two countries, but it will do for our purposes here. Therefore, any attempt to solve the problem of defining income by saying that one should simply transplant 'Western' tax laws raises the immediate query: which of the various tax laws does one choose?

Countries differ widely in the particular case of capital gains taxes e.g. Guyana and Puerto Rico have sophisticated arrangements for taxing gains at different rates according to the length of time for which assets have been held, whereas Malaysia made an abortive effort to introduce legislation in 1965 but it never in fact reached the statute book. The trend in India since independence has been to move away from the British tradition towards a more inclusive concept including capital gains and income in kind.

Even if there were a fully agreed set of definitions in 'Western' countries, it would be wrong to apply them to African and similar territories without further thought. There are at least two fundamental difficulties arising from the presence of many subsistence farmers (i.e. farmers supplying their own needs) and the differing nature of transfer payments and income-creating transactions.

In 'Western' countries, it is not usually a matter of very great consequence if one does not tax income in kind e.g. that derived from farm production for own consumption. The importance of output of this sort, either in relation to total farm incomes or to the national income, is such that no great harm is likely to be done whatever decisions are adopted. But in underdeveloped countries, the position may be very different in so far as subsistence output is of overwhelming importance in the economy. Therefore one must have a clear-cut view on whether or not to include it in income.

National income statisticians have argued out this subject over the years and most of them would probably now agree that a national income total which does not include subsistence output is unacceptable. This is certainly the view I have taken in the past myself[1] and there would not seem to be any obvious reason for changing it. But this does not finally dispose of the problem: even though it is agreed that subsistence output comes under the general heading of income, should one necessarily conclude that it should suffer income tax? After all, the argument runs, a subsistence producer by definition earns no cash and so how can he pay tax if he has no cash income?

This line of argument does not seem to be a valid generalisation. First of all, there is an important distinction between those who are *partly* and those who are *purely* subsistence producers; in many of the most backward parts of Africa one seems to find some cash element in economic life however irregular and however unimportant compared to the subsistence element. Secondly, even if we hypothesise a man who has no cash income, it does not follow that he has no cash. The extensive system of primitive social security which one finds in some countries often results in transfers from the more to the less prosperous members of a family group. The transfers may not be in cash form; and the pure subsistence farmers may not receive them. But there is a strong likelihood that in one way or another many ostensibly subsistence families do handle cash in the course of each year. On these grounds therefore one must reject the view that the imputed income from subsistence output should, as a matter of principle, be kept out of range of income taxation. There are other reasons why it is difficult or undesirable – and some why it is desirable – to tax subsistence income but we are not dealing with these points at the moment.

Some major difficulties of definition are raised when we consider the dividing line between transfers and transactions – or unilateral and bilateral flows, as the jargon goes. In African territories one meets all sorts of payments – bribes, gratuities, remittances to relatives, tribal subscriptions, contributions for communal purposes – which defy easy analysis. One can, of course, apply the usual tests and ask whether a transaction is legal

---

[1] *Cf.* A. R. Prest and I. G. Stewart, *The National Income of Nigeria, 1950–1* (HMSO, London, 1953), and A. R. Prest, *The Investigation of National Income in British Tropical Dependencies* (Athlone Press, London, 1957).

or illegal, whether there is any *quid pro quo* corresponding to a money flow and so on. But one usually does not get very far on this tack. How, for instance, does one classify the bribe accepted by an interpreter to put a case better in an African court of law? Any such payment may be technically illegal but on the other hand it is highly likely to affect the enthusiasm of the interpreter and the skill and verve with which he presents his case. Examples of this sort could easily be multiplied but we shall have made our point if we simply say that there are many snags of income definition in many countries which are logically prior to those found in the assessment and collection of income taxes. Unless one is alive to the inherent difficulties of this sort, one cannot hope to have a full understanding of these matters.

We now come to the assessment of income. If an income tax is to be anything other than a poll tax – or at the most a tax based on occupation or profession – some attempt at assessment of individual incomes becomes necessary. This immediately raises serious difficulties in many underdeveloped countries. The first is that even the measurement of income of a group of people may be extraordinarily difficult when weights and measures are far from standardised,[1] when one has either an illiterate peasantry which is incapable of keeping accounts or a semi-illiterate group which is unwilling to do so,[2] and when a large proportion of output is not exchanged in the market for money (and to the extent that when money transactions do occur they are in cash rather than credit form). It makes an enormous difference whether one values output which is bartered or used for subsistence purposes on a retail or an ex-farm basis. As has been maintained elsewhere, the balance of the argument would seem to be in favour of the former.[3]

[1] *Cf.* A. R. Prest and I. G. Stewart, *op. cit.*, Appendix C, for a discussion of these matters in Nigeria. One of the 'standard' measures in the Northern Region, a *mudu*, was found to have at least thirteen different interpretations, depending on the commodity concerned.

[2] Even further complexities are said to arise in such areas as Malaysia and Singapore, where one has to grapple with the mysteries of Chinese accounting, as well as the unwillingness of local businessmen to distinguish between business and personal transactions.

[3] A. R. Prest and I. G. Stewart, *op. cit.*, pp. 12–15.

Nor is this all. For even if one can evaluate the income of a producer group during any period, the allocation of this income (which may not be in cash form) between the different members of the group may well need the wisdom of Solomon.

Of course, this does not imply that only underdeveloped countries run into problems of this kind. It has always been more difficult to levy income tax in countries with a large number[1] of primary producers (e.g. France) and so it is not surprising to find the same issues, albeit in more accentuated form, in the largely primary producing countries with which we are concerned here.

We now come to the fixing of tax rates and allowances. Can it be said that the authorities have failed to develop the yield of personal income taxation because they have failed to apply the appropriate rates of tax? Martin and Lewis have argued[2] that this is so, for the following reason. If one applies the tax rates found in the UK to, say Ghana or Nigeria, it makes all the difference in the world whether they are applied at the same absolute level of income or at the same relative level of income as in the UK. Supposing, for instance, that a man earning £500 a year in the UK pays 5% of his income in tax and a man earning £1,000 pays 15%. Then one will not get the same ratio of tax revenue to income in a poor country as in the UK if one applies these rates as they stand, for the simple reason that the proportion of total income in these ranges is far less in a poorer country. More formally, we can say that if we have a series of tax rates a, b, c . . . applying to the first, second, third . . . percentiles of incomes in the UK, then if we are to have the same ratio of tax yield to income in, say, Nigeria, the same tax rates must apply to the same percentiles of income in that country. It should be noted that the argument runs in terms of *incomes* and not *numbers of incomes*. For if incomes were less unequally distributed in the poorer country than in the richer one, the

---

[1] It is, of course, the number of producers rather than the volume of production which is the critical factor.

[2] A. M. Martin and W. A. Lewis, 'Patterns of Public Revenue and Expenditure', *Manchester School*, September 1956, p. 223; and also W. A. Lewis, *Development Planning* (Allen and Unwin, London, 1966), p. 124.

proportion of income accruing to the upper percentiles of the number of recipients would be less and the proportion to lower percentiles greater. Hence the application of the same rates of tax on the basis of numbers rather than incomes would result in a lower overall tax/income ratio than in the richer country. The converse would follow if income were more unequally distributed in the poorer country. So the general argument must be in terms of amounts of income rather than numbers of income recipients.

Such is the logic of the argument. Although it has been cast in terms of tax rates, it obviously applies, *mutatis mutandis*, to the size of income tax allowances; both should be geared to the level of incomes in the country in which they are applied rather than to that in the 'parent' country. As an example, we can quote Professor Shoup's recommendation that the exemption limit for personal income tax in Liberia be reduced from the level of $1,500 at which it stood in 1969.[1] Measures of the kind adopted in Ghana in recent years to restrict income tax allowances also fall into this category, but we shall have more to say about these shortly.

There can be no doubt that in the past many underdeveloped countries have at most followed the practices of richer countries with respect to income tax rates and allowances and sometimes, depending on the balance of political forces, have not even done as much as that.[2] And there can equally be no doubt that so long as they do this it is quite impossible for them to have a similar tax/income ratio. Whether they should apply the same tax rates to the same percentiles of income as in richer countries is another matter. There are at least two points here which

[1] C. S. Shoup *et al.*, *The Tax System of Liberia* (Columbia University Press, 1970). It is also important to avoid setting precedents such as the exemption of particular organisations and activities which are not only difficult to remove themselves but may also lead to claims for similar treatment by like organisations. *Cf.* C. T. Edwards, *op. cit.*, p. 135, for an example in Malaysia.

[2] A number of observers have noted that the ratio of the income tax exemption limit to income per head is often higher in developing than in developed countries. See e.g. C. S. Shoup *et al.*, *The Fiscal System of Venezuela* (Johns Hopkins, Baltimore, 1959), p. 93n; *Economic Survey of Asia and the Far East*, 1960 (UN, Bangkok, 1961), p. 94; E. A. Arowolo, 'The Taxation of Low Incomes in African Countries', *IMF Staff Papers*, July, 1968.

must make one hesitate: first, there are the administrative problems of collecting taxes from large numbers of people in poor countries and, second, there is the matter of incentives. It will be convenient to deal with this administrative question when we come to the general subject of collection and so we can begin with the incentives issue.

The general theoretical arguments here are well known – the opposing income and substitution effects and the ramifications of group as opposed to individual effects – and so we need not dwell on them. The special point to make here is that, as far as incentives to work are concerned, we not only have to look at the choice between work and leisure, but also between non-taxed work and taxed work. However good the income tax organisation in a country, some kinds of activity always escape tax, or at any rate pay less than their full share of tax. In advanced countries, people can in general choose between more spare-time jobs (painting one's own house) and more time at the factory, and married women in particular can retire from the labour market altogether and devote themselves to household work. In underdeveloped countries, there is often[1] a choice between untaxed or partially taxed subsistence production and output for sale in the monetised sector. The possibility that a tax structure may force people back into the subsistence sector or in any way retard the growth of the cash sector is not one to be faced with equanimity in any of these countries. We know far too little about people's responses to changes in the (net) reward per unit of work at the margin in any country to be dogmatic and lay down the law. But it would nevertheless be extremely surprising if it were possible to levy income taxes in the manner suggested above without very considerable repercussions, and adverse repercussions, on the structure of the private sector of the economy whatever the merits of the public expenditure made possible by any additional yield from taxation. This would seem especially likely in a country like Ceylon where (in 1971) the combination of income tax and various other imposts was

[1] Though not always, e.g. if the menfolk are mainly responsible for cash crop production and the womenfolk for subsistence output.

such as to make the marginal rate of tax 100 % or thereabouts in some cases. And if the repercussions take the form of riots or insurrections – as is not unknown – the consequences for output and development may be more serious still. On *a priori* grounds, the same arguments are likely to apply in respect of incentives to save, but we shall deal more fully with this matter later.

We now come to matters of tax collection. The first point here is that some of the technical devices used in Western countries, and notably that of collection of tax at source, are only of limited application. Where it has been possible to introduce systems of Pay-As-You-Earn there have been spectacular increases in the numbers of tax-payers and the tax collected (e.g. the income tax history of Jamaica in the 1950s) but in the nature of things one cannot apply these devices to peasant and similarly independent producers, so one would expect considerable inequity on this account. Secondly, opportunities for evasion are naturally easy; what *does* one do in an African territory about income tax defaulters who retreat into the bush or over unguarded frontiers or about those who regard prisons as rather good rest houses? Income tax authorities in most countries have relied much more on the co-operation of the taxpayer than is usually admitted. Or, putting the same point slightly differently, no income tax system can be expected to work effectively unless there is a situation of mutual respect between taxpayers and tax officials – as Professor Hart has emphasised in the context of Latin America.[1] At the same time – and we now come to another point – there can be no doubt that in many territories the administration of income tax even at the rates currently prevailing has left a great deal to be desired. Determination to prosecute offenders and willingness to expose them could very frequently make an immense amount of difference to the efficiency with which income tax affairs are conducted[2] instead of leaving tax declarations as exercises in poetic

[1] A. G. Hart, 'Fiscal Policy in Latin America', *Journal of Political Economy*, July–August 1970, *Supplement*.

[2] I once had occasion to point out to the officials of a territory that there were more cars than income tax payers in it. The answer was that they failed to see the relevance of the remark!

41

imagination, to use Professor Hart's phraseology. It is not so much a matter of introducing new penalties for non-payment – tax laws are not usually deficient in such respects[1] – but simply of enforcing them. The critical importance of insisting on prompt tax collection in an inflationary context is also insufficiently recognised. Continued delays in collection imply not only permanent but also growing interest free loans to taxpayers in such circumstances.[2] But all too often the manifold pressures to turn a blind eye on tax delinquents are too strong for weak or inexperienced administrators. It must be expected that such pressures – and for that matter all the difficulties of collecting income taxes – would be far greater if the income tax system were re-cast on the lines suggested above.

We conclude therefore that there are four main reasons why income tax yield is so low in these countries – problems of defining income, problems of assessing and measuring it, the choice of rates and allowances and the difficulties of tax collection. Perhaps we can finish this section with one last observation. The conversion of income tax into a mass tax was not something which happened easily and smoothly in either the UK or the USA. In both cases, it needed the shock and stimulus of wartime conditions to bring about the change. Unless and until the inhabitants of underdeveloped countries – and their political representatives – can be made to feel that it is just as important for them to have a mass income tax to finance government expenditure as the UK and USA felt it was important for war finance, the possibility of any sudden and sweeping change in this respect is not very great. This is not saying that no important changes will take place – the post-war history of income tax in Nigeria[3] is evidence to the contrary – but simply that it would be unwise to set one's sights too high in these matters.

---

[1] Cf. H. W. T. Pepper and J. C. L. Huiskamy, 'Guilt and Innocence of Taxpayers', *Bulletin of International Fiscal Documentation*, November 1969. At the same time one might not wish to support some countries' devices, e.g. the exemption from tax of rewards to informers.

[2] Cf. Hart, *op. cit.*, also R. M. Bird, *Public Finance and Economic Development* (Harvard University Press, Cambridge, Mass., 1970), p. 60 ff.

[3] Cf. A. Adedeji, 'The Future of Personal Income Taxation in Nigeria',

INCOME TAX CHILDREN'S ALLOWANCES

To begin a discussion on this subject we must pose the question whether general principles of equity can give a clear-cut answer to the tax treatment of families *vis-à-vis* single individuals or childless married couples. It is possible to think of two extreme positions. First, one can simply say that the decision to have a child rather than, say, a durable consumer good is a matter of choice for parents. If one set of parents decided on the former, why should it receive greater tax allowances than another making the second choice? The second extreme position is to regard every member of a family as a separate entity for tax purposes, so that a family of, say, three will pay the same amount of tax as the sum of tax paid by three single people each earning one-third of the aggregate income of the family. There are obvious difficulties of equating children and adults in any such formulation (e.g. should all children, whatever their age, be regarded as representing the same fraction of an adult?), but the general point holds that these two extremes represent substantially different tax positions for any given family facing a system of progressive taxation.[1]

Can either of these two extremes be defended on grounds of equity? To simplify the problem, let us assume that the child members of a family do not have any income of their own. In this case, it can be argued with conviction that the first extreme position (i.e. no child allowances whatever) is untenable. Irrespective of whether one thinks that this is or is not just as between parents with children and those without, some injustice would clearly be done to the children themselves. One can be quite safe in saying that they have no choice in deciding whether to be born or not! Nor does the second extreme position carry much more conviction. Although there are some valid, or

Nigerian Journal of Economic and Social Studies, July 1965. Interesting experiments have also been made in other countries in levying rough and ready income taxes at local levels.

[1] If taxation is strictly proportional to income, then it obviously does not matter whether total family income is split among the constituent members for tax purposes or not.

partly valid, arguments when we consider the comparative position of single individuals and married couples (e.g. why should a married couple pay any more in tax than two single individuals living together with the same aggregate income?) there is nothing comparable in respect of children. The simple point is that they are not separate individuals divorced from their families and so it would be entirely artificial to establish a tax system which pretends that they are.

It would seem, therefore, that abstract considerations of equity suggest that some tax allowances should be granted in respect of children but these do not enable us to settle the details with finality in cases where the juvenile members of a family have no income of their own. Is the position different if children do have income of their own? In the case of unearned income, the answer would seem to be still the same i.e. there is no case for treating children as separate units but, equally, one cannot ignore their existence altogether. If children earn income, on the other hand, the general principle should be to treat them as separate individuals once they have reached the age of discretion and become self-supporting, but to be prepared to aggregate their incomes with family income if they have not. The 'age of discretion' is a vague notion to which it may only be possible to give clear meaning in the context of a particular country at a particular time, but it is good enough for our purposes.

If there is no clear-cut solution in equity to these questions we are forced to the conclusion that tax allowances for children in any country must depend on general economic and social policy. As far as underdeveloped countries are concerned this immediately brings us to population policy. Opinions can legitimately differ about the influence of financial considerations on birth rates. But unless and until it can be shown that such factors have no effects at all, it seems necessary to discuss them. It may well be that more direct measures – birth control propaganda etc – will be far more effective than financial ones; but as a minimum it would seem desirable that the latter should not pull in the wrong direction.

We talked about the facts of population growth in Chapter 1 and all we need say again on this topic is that in many countries economic development is retarded much more than it would be if the rate of growth of population were less. Given that general background, it must therefore follow that from this angle children's allowances for tax purposes ought to be on a niggardly rather than a generous basis. A more refined policy would aim at a structure of allowances which was such that the tax savings in having larger families varied as between income groups in such a way that tax remissions were relatively smaller in those income groups with the highest crude birth rates. This is, no doubt, too much to ask for as a general policy proposition but may be kept in mind as a background ideal.

So much for abstract considerations. What do we actually find in practice? Historically, children's allowances in ex-British territories have been made in a form similar to those in the UK income-tax system i.e. children (and their income, if any) are aggregated with the parents and lump-sum deductions are made from gross parental income to arrive at taxable income. If we compare this system with that of the 'quotient' system[1] found in France, we find that if both systems treat a family relatively to a married couple in exactly the same way at a low point in the income scale, the quotient system is considerably more favourable at the higher income ranges. If the quotient system is somewhat more favourable at the lower income ranges it is considerably more favourable at the higher income ranges. If it were thought necessary on population policy grounds to discriminate relatively more against lower income groups, there might, therefore, be some advantage in the French rather than the British system. But, as we have said, this is an exotic sort of notion, and in any case, the likelihood is that the quotient system would be more generous than the British even at low income levels. Therefore, this line of thought does not look very helpful.

[1] E.g. a family of four 'equivalent adults' (each child being counted as half an adult) pays as much tax as the total amount paid by four adults each having one quarter of the family's income.

What do we find from a comparison of children's allowances in developing countries with those in the UK? Whereas in the UK the ratio of dependants, allowances for a family of four (two adults, two children) to a family of two adults is approximately 1.7 (taking the family of two as 1.0) we find that the corresponding figures for Jamaica and Mauritius are 1.4 and 1.3, the precise figure in each case depending on the children's ages. Of course, the amount of actual tax remission secured by these allowances at any given income level depends on the tax rate structure. But so far as these examples go, they do suggest that in two territories faced with rapidly growing populations, the relationship to the British pattern is of the right general kind – there would be much more to criticise if the ratio were greater than that found in the UK.

However, too much stress should not be laid on isolated examples and, in particular, no one should jump to the conclusion that there are no changes to be made anywhere. Professor Meade came to the conclusion some years ago in his study of Mauritius[1] that on grounds of population policy no income tax allowances should be given for any child beyond the third. This kind of policy has now been adopted in a number of countries, e.g. in Kenya, the maximum number of children for which allowances can be claimed is four. And in Ghana there is a standard income tax allowance for dependants regardless of number. Another possibility is to grant generous relief on married women's earnings. We cannot discuss the ins and outs of the correct income tax treatment of married women's earnings, but suffice it to say that on grounds of general population policy (and economic incentives as well, for that matter) there is a field of inquiry here which cannot be lightly ignored.

It is sometimes argued that as personal income taxation only applies to a relatively small section of the population in many underdeveloped countries, these sorts of details are not worth fussing about. It is surely just as legitimate to argue that it is important to sort out these arrangements before it applies to a lot of people, as seems to be the intention in some countries.

[1] *Op. cit.*, p. 165.

46

It is usually easier to prevent a vested interest arising than to try to eradicate it once it is established. One other point should also be made. Even if an income tax system were such as to be highly favourable to many-children families, it would, in principle, be possible to offset such benefits in some if not in all cases, by a suitable system of indirect taxes, i.e. one which differentiates against families with children. Needless to say, such a system would be difficult to contrive in practice. The point is simply that the overall tax treatment of families with children depends on the structure of indirect as well as of direct taxes.

Lastly, we must take into account the possibility that liberal income tax allowances may have beneficial effects on productivity in so far as they enable existing children in large families to develop into more fully productive members of the labour force than would otherwise be the case.[1] If this is so, there is then a real clash of economic interests, between keeping down the rate of growth of a population and making the best use of that which one already has. The solution of any such dilemma must depend on the particular circumstances of a country – how far the income tax system reaches down to the lower income levels, whether the difference between 'liberal' and 'niggardly' allowances can be sufficient to influence the birth rate without being so much as to affect productivity, what alternative policy instruments exist, and so on.

COMPANY TAXATION[2]

Initially we shall confine ourselves to the major problems arising in the taxation of company profits, assuming that these can be looked at in isolation. Subsequently we shall be concerned with two other very important topics: special incentives to business enterprise and the integration of company and personal taxation.

[1] *Cf.* C. S. Shoup, 'Production from Consumption', *Public Finance*, Parts 1 and 2, 1965; and also his *Public Finance* (Weidenfeld and Nicolson, London, 1969), pp. 592–4.

[2] For a more detailed treatment of these problems in one particular part of the world see A. R. Prest, 'Corporate Income Taxation in Latin America', Organisation of American States (Joint Tax Program), *Fiscal Policy for Economic Growth in Latin America* (Johns Hopkins, Baltimore, 1965).

There are some obvious arguments in favour of raising a large amount by way of company taxation in underdeveloped countries. The first is the ease of collection. Companies are easily identifiable, keep accounts and cannot escape tax liabilities by, for instance, rapid changes of their place of residence. In these respects they are almost an administrator's dream. A further point is that taxes collected in this way often appear 'painless'. At the very least, it might be argued that the overt repercussions of collecting a given sum of tax direct from a company will be much less than if collected from the shareholders of the company, or for that matter from any other group of individuals. 'Repercussions' have in this context not only economic but also political overtones – in the sense that individuals have votes but companies do not. In the circumstances, it is not surprising that, however lax the tax authorities are with personal income tax and however low the rates, they rarely fail to levy company taxes at rates which are comparable with those found in Western countries.

Despite these obvious advantages, there are nevertheless some tight constraints on the freedom of manoeuvre of underdeveloped countries in this field. First, there is the point that company income is often only a small part of GNP in many countries. There are two reasons for this: first, the sectors in which companies usually predominate (e.g. heavy industry) are relatively less important and secondly, the role of incorporated businesses is relatively smaller inside any given sector (e.g. small traders rather than department stores). There are some notable exceptions, especially the oil economies, but this proposition does nevertheless hold for many countries.[1] In addition, there are some very strong reasons why tax rates on companies cannot be pushed too high. Although they may appear 'painless' to the administrator with his eye fixed on short-run reactions, it

---

[1] The differing importance of manufacturing industry, etc in East African countries has been a major reason for company taxation being a much greater fraction of GNP in Kenya than in other East African territories (*cf.* N. Jetha, 'Company Taxation in East Africa', *British Tax Review*, Jan.–Feb. 1965).

would be a bold man who would deny that incentives to existing companies to take risks in investment are impaired by high company taxes. And if it is argued that higher taxes would frequently be paid out of undistributed profits rather than dividends, this invites the riposte that taxation will not release real resources but only cut down saving by the private sector.[1] In fact, many countries have in recent years made very considerable concessions to companies in the form of tax holidays, accelerated depreciation and so on. As we shall be dealing with these matters shortly we need not go further into them at this stage. The point which is relevant here is that if specially low tax rates are being levied on some companies it would appear very inequitable to levy specially high taxes on others.

Nor is it just a matter of the effects on companies already in being. High company tax rates may discourage the formation of new companies and thereby retard the growth of joint-stock enterprise.[2] Furthermore, the absence of the fear of competition from new companies may very well strengthen tendencies to monopoly or oligopoly among existing companies – tendencies which are not usually in need of strengthening.

There is one particular facet of the incentives argument which merits further examination. In recent years, the rapid extension of Double Taxation Agreements has done much to prevent double taxation of companies operating in more than one country. In particular, as company tax rates have remained at high levels in such major capital exporting countries as the USA and the UK, it has often been possible for underdeveloped territories to levy substantial taxes on the profits of American and British companies without affecting their total tax liability – the higher taxation abroad simply serving to reduce net tax

[1] Such savings may, however, be used for investment in other countries and so not be available for domestic purposes.

[2] The converse problem, that very low rates of tax may encourage company formation to escape the full rigours of personal income taxation is far less important in most developing countries.

liability at home. But this state of affairs ceases to hold once underdeveloped country tax rates rise to or above the rates found in the UK and the USA – and at even lower levels in so far as expatriate companies are for one reason or another not liable to tax at home on profits retained abroad. There is, therefore, a definite limit to which tax rates on foreign companies can be raised in underdeveloped countries without serious risk of repelling foreign capital. And if there are limits to practicable tax rates on foreign companies, this very frequently sets limits to tax rates applied to home companies.

Many other problems arise with company taxation. The assessment of profits in a highly inflationary situation involves questions of the appropriate treatment of depreciation and inventories. In one country at least (Chile, 1964) the rough and ready compensation was to make an arbitrary cut in profits as customarily calculated. Another perpetual difficulty is the correct valuation of imports of goods and services used by expatriate companies; it is not unknown for these to be overvalued so as to reduce corporate tax liability in the developing country and, even more important, by-pass exchange controls on dividends to head offices. Rate structures are also frequently defective in various ways. Sometimes it is a case of levying progressive taxes on corporations, a procedure which ignores the possibility of rich men owning small companies and poor men owning large ones; sometimes tax differentiation which is justified, for instance on bearer shares, is not practised. At other times (e.g. India, Colombia) there have been attempts to levy a multiplicity of taxes on corporations, including such normally unjustified components as excess profits taxes.[1] It is all too easy to lose sight of the cumulative harmful effects of a whole array of taxes of this sort. Company tax law is bound to be complicated; but there is no excuse at all for making it unnecessarily so.

[1] There may be occasional exceptions, e.g. when a company is given a franchise, but there is difficulty in estimating prospective profits. An excess profits tax arrangement can then be a second line of defence.

TAX RELIEF AND SUBSIDIES TO ENTERPRISE[1]

This topic is not susceptible to neat classification. It has claims
to come in either a revenue or an expenditure chapter; and
claims to come in either this revenue chapter or the next one;
and claims to be associated with either personal or company
taxation. On balance, it seems best to deal with it at this point
in the narrative as it is more closely connected with company
taxation than any other topic but it must be confessed that there
is a certain element of arbitrariness in this decision.

Aid of this kind may take a wide variety of forms – help in
capital investment (either by subsidies or special depreciation
provisions), remission of income tax for a limited period, subsidies on outputs (or inputs), protective tariffs and so on. All
these devices have been tried at different times by different
countries and frequently more than one at a time. Their general
outlines are well known and we shall not attempt to describe
their operation in detail in particular countries. Instead, we
shall concentrate on analysing the rationale of each method and
subsequently compare their relative merits.

The usual methods of encouraging investment are to allow
accelerated depreciation or to grant an investment subsidy.
Accelerated depreciation frequently takes the form of allowing
a (new) firm to write off the cost of its capital investment in a
short period e.g. five years.[2] Sometimes it is also provided that
normal wear and tear allowances should be given in addition
in this period, but logically we then step over the borderline
from accelerated depreciation to investment subsidies and so it is
convenient to keep these two devices separate in our discussion.

The fundamental point about accelerated depreciation is that
it postpones some tax liabilities into the future and, therefore,

[1] For more detailed treatment see A. R. Prest, 'Taxes, Subsidies and Investment
Incentives' in A. T. Peacock (ed.) *Government Finance and Economic Development*
(OECD, Paris, 1965); and 'Fiscal Measures and Capital Accumulation' in
A. N. Agarwala and S. P. Singh (ed.), *Accelerating Investment in Developing
Economies* (Oxford University Press, Oxford, 1969).

[2] E.g. the Jamaican legislation allows pioneer manufacturers to write off 20%
p.a. over a five-year period, the relevant years being any five out of the first eight
years after incurring the expenditure.

51

the taxpayer benefits by the value of the compound interest on this postponement. The precise benefit to any individual tax-payer will depend on the amount of tax postponed, the length of the period concerned and the relevant rate of interest. As the effective length of period will depend on the rate of growth of a firm's capital stock (i.e. successive new investments may in effect prolong the period of tax remission) and the appropriate rate of interest may vary enormously from one firm to another, the calculation of benefits may be a complicated matter. Post-ponement of tax liability influences investment in two ways: first, it increases the ability of firms to expand by increasing the liquid assets at their disposal, and second, it reduces the riski-ness of capital investment. Of these, the second is probably the more important. We shall not go into the details of this encourage-ment to take risks as it has been discussed at some length else-where[1] but the essential point is that in the limiting case of 100 % initial allowances (i.e. the total cost of an asset being written off in the first year) we have a situation equivalent to a zero tax rate. Hence any net discrimination against risky enter-prises inherent in the usual income tax arrangements is removed; if only part of the original cost can be written off in the first year, discrimination against risk is only partially removed. In the somewhat unlikely eventuality that losses can be completely and immediately offset against other profits, the picture is some-what different. For in this case we should find that a proportional income tax without initial allowances would favour risk-taking relatively to one with 100 % initial allowances; the latter, being a zero-rate tax, does not reduce either the mean or the variance of the return from an investment, when expressed as a fraction of the capital contributed by the investor, i.e. there is no tax on rewards when lucky but also no compensation for losses when unlucky. But we shall become deeply involved in this if we go any further; all we need to say now is that one can more usually expect accelerated depreciation to lead to some diminu-tion in the riskiness of investment.

[1] R. A. Musgrave, *op. cit.*, pp. 343–4; and C. S. Shoup, *Public Finance, op. cit.*, Ch. 12.

Investment subsidies, the system whereby firms are allowed to write off wear and tear in the usual way but are, in addition, given a subsidy proportional to the cost of capital investment, have somewhat different effects. If an investment subsidy of 20% is compared with an initial allowance of 20% and the normal wear and tear allowance for the first year is claimable in both cases, the effects on the liquidity position of a firm and its *ability* to invest will be identical, the same tax relief being given in both cases at the date of making the investment.[1] But as far as *incentives* to invest are concerned the position will differ: in the initial allowance case, total wear and tear allowances do not exceed 100% of cost, whereas in the investment subsidy case they do and so it must follow that in the years after Year 1, the latter is more beneficial to a firm[2] and hence will encourage investment more than the former. This is a rather hastily sketched picture of the differences between the two systems but it may suffice to bring out the essential points.

Another means of encouraging new industries is to grant a tax holiday for a given period. The length of the period varies from one country to another, e.g. Antigua 5 years, Trinidad 5–10 years and Jamaica 10–15 years (in some circumstances). Some countries allow firms to choose within limits the individual years in which the concession may be claimed, rather than confining it to the first in years of operation. Dividends paid during these years may also be tax free (e.g. Nigeria).

A tax holiday provides the same general sort of incentives as accelerated depreciation or investment subsidies. If a firm makes any profits in the early years of life, it will enjoy greater liquidity than in the absence of this concession. It is also likely to diminish the risk of new investment in so far as the effective rate of tax on profits is reduced. Indeed, the general advantages of this type

---

[1] There may be some difference if for any reason one type of allowance can only be claimed later than the other. There are also other differences, depending on whether the subsidy takes the form of an outright grant or, as assumed here, a deduction against taxes on profits.

[2] *Cf.* J. Heller and K. F. Kauffman, *Tax Incentives in Less Developed Countries* (Harvard Law School (International Program on Taxation), Cambridge, Mass., 1963), for detailed explanations.

of concession can best be thought of as being equivalent to a permanent reduction (as distinct from temporary abolition) of the rate of tax on profits. But even if the incentives are of the same general character, they obviously differ a good deal in detail. Whereas accelerated depreciation etc concessions depend on the rate of investment in fixed capital, in the tax holiday case the basic determinant is the level of profits. This contrast points to some important differences, as we shall see shortly.

An entirely different system for granting tax relief to new enterprises is to manipulate indirect taxes and subsidies. This can take a number of different forms. Imported materials and/or capital equipment can be relieved of import duty. A protective tariff can be imposed on imports of selected goods from abroad. A subsidy can be paid in one form or another to firms on the basis of turnover. All these devices have the same general purpose, that of promoting internal consumption of the favoured commodities. The first and the third will also directly help to promote sales abroad. There are so many examples in so many countries of these various techniques that no more need be said about them in explanation.

What can be said of the comparative merits of all these various devices? There are a number of rather intricate and important ways in which they differ, but before we examine them we must deal with one point which is sometimes raised. It is sometimes argued that a tariff is superior to a tax holiday because the former adds to government revenue whilst the latter reduces it. This line of reasoning would seem to be incomplete. A general principle of tax analysis is that to assess the relative merits of different fiscal devices one must assume the same degree of budget balance in both cases, i.e. if one is comparing two taxes, one must assume an equal revenue yield or, if one is asking about the effects of raising more revenue from one tax, one must also ask what additional expenditure takes place as a result of the tax. Viewed in this light there is clearly nothing in the argument above, except in the case when a tariff turns the terms of trade in favour of the country imposing it. Let us leave this point on one side and focus on the basic issue by postulating an economy with two industries, A and B. Policy 1 would involve a subsidy to industry A financed by a poll tax; policy 2 would raise the same amount of revenue by taxing the products of industry B, the proceeds being distributed in lump sum grants per head. There would be nothing to choose between these policies from a resource allocation standpoint; but clearly the first is analogous to a tax holiday for domestic industry and the second to a tariff on imports. This may seem – and indeed is – a trite point but it is necessary to make it in view of the misconceptions which persist on these matters.

Suppose we now compare the relative effects of the tax holiday and the accelerated depreciation (or investment subsidy) methods. In the one case, tax remissions are related to profits and, in the other, to fixed capital investment. In the accelerated depreciation case, two firms – subject to the same rate of profits tax and with the same credit rating – may purchase identical pieces of capital equipment in any given year; they will gain exactly the same amounts from the concession, in the sense that the present value of the tax deferment will be the same in both cases. In the tax holiday case, on the other hand, if one firm earns a higher rate of return on any given fixed capital investment than the other, it will receive a greater benefit from the concession. Finally, if the ratio of fixed to working capital differs between the two firms, then even though the rate of return be the same on all capital investment, the firm with the higher ratio of working to fixed capital will receive relatively more benefit in the tax holiday case.

How much difference there is between the accelerated depreciation/investment subsidy and the tax holiday approaches in their encouragement of capital-intensive methods of production has been a matter for argument in the past. Essentially, a tax on income but with 100 % initial allowances amounts to a zero rate tax on profits whereas a tax holiday amounts to a temporary exemption of profits from tax. Thus we should expect the former to offer relatively greater encouragement to use capital-intensive methods, but the precise difference in any particular case will clearly depend on whether initial allowances are 100 % or less and on how long the tax holiday lasts. The cheapening of the cost of capital implied in accelerated depreciation etc produces both a bias in favour of capitalistic methods of production inside any one firm and relatively greater encouragement to those industries which are more than normally capital-intensive. This is obviously a point of great importance for employment and output levels in countries which are relatively poorly endowed with capital and relatively well endowed with labour resources.[1] Indeed, the Meade inquiry in Mauritius decided on these grounds to recommend the abolition of investment (though not initial) allowances in that territory.[2]

On one other point allowances based on capital investment may be deemed superior to those related to profits. In the one case, the size of the tax remission depends on the rate of investment and, in the other, on the level of profits. Both these bases are likely to fluctuate with the level of income. Of the two, the latter is less amenable to any form of government control (investment can always be regulated by licensing of various kinds) and, therefore, may be deemed more of an 'open-ended' commitment over which the ministry of finance has less control.[3] This is more a point of budgetary procedure and management but it must be made in this context as well as in that of Chapter 7.

Accelerated depreciation differs from investment allowances or subsidies in that it is of relatively greater value to firms purchasing long-lived capital equipment, tax deferment then being effectively granted for a longer period of time. In the case of investment allowances the answer is complicated but the most likely result is that there will be no bias one way or the other. So if investment and initial allowances are arranged to give equal tax benefits in respect of investment goods of average durability, the former will be relatively more beneficial for goods of less than average length of life and relatively less so for goods of more than average life.

[1] A. R. Prest, *Fiscal Survey of the British Caribbean* (HMSO, 1957), pp. 27–8.
[2] *Op. cit.*, p. 162.
[3] Estimates of revenue lost by concessions of the sorts discussed seem to range between 2% and 10% of total revenue (cf.G. E. Lent, 'Tax Incentives in Developing Countries', *Rivista di Diritto Finanziario e Scienza delle Finanze*, March 1970).

As far as the various devices of exempting imported materials, taxing imports etc are concerned, there is less to say in terms of economic analysis. The usual arguments about the merits of direct and indirect taxation, and of subsidies and grants have to be seen in the context of a deliberate intention to change the allocation of resources. The relevant sorts of economic issues are, therefore, the elasticities of home and foreign demand and supply with respect to changes in relative market prices of home-produced and foreign varieties of goods. The relevant kinds of administrative issues, just as with accelerated depreciation or the tax holiday case, are how one selects the favoured commodities, and how one finally gets away from a system of subsidising home production whether directly or indirectly. Finally, it must be stressed that these ways of aiding firms will help to reduce the size of losses, whereas liberalised depreciation and tax holidays usually only yield immediate benefits to firms actually making profits.

One further point needs to be mentioned. In so far as local income or profits tax concessions are made to foreign companies, these may be completely nullified by the operation of Double Taxation Relief agreements. Thus if the developed country tax rate on companies is 50% and that in the underdeveloped is reduced, say, to 25% on certain companies, this may simply have the effect of reducing the tax revenue of the latter and increasing that of the former. It should be noted that exactly the same applies with liberal depreciation provisions in an underdeveloped territory if a foreign company is taxed at home on the basis of 'ordinary' depreciation allowances. There are circumstances in which tax concessions really will be effective. One is when there is a wide-ranging exemption of income from abroad from tax (e.g. Canada or the Netherlands) or where there is special legislation of the type which prevailed in the UK between 1957 and 1965.[1] A second is where a Double Taxation Agreement not only allows a credit for foreign income

[1] UK companies were allowed to establish Overseas Trade Corporations for certain overseas activities; these were exempt from UK tax in respect of retained profits.

tax against domestic tax but also incorporates a tax-sparing clause, whereby relief is given not for actual tax paid abroad but for the tax which would have been paid, had there not been special concessions such as tax holidays and the like. Various agreements on these lines have been made in recent years between the UK and other countries. Double Taxation Agreements can also provide for the exemption of inward income from domestic tax. Finally, some developing countries (e.g. Jamaica, Trinidad) tax income remitted abroad at different rates, depending on the tax treatment in the receiving country.[1] Where none of these reliefs apply, the methods of subsidy or differential taxation of imports are superior to tax holidays or liberal depreciation. In so far as gross profits before tax increase due to subsidies etc, a foreign firm will only lose a proportion of the increase (depending on the tax rate) and not the total amount as is the case when gross profits are unchanged but depreciation allowances are liberalised.

One or two final reflections may be in order on these contentious issues. First of all, concessions of the types we have described must almost inevitably discriminate in favour of some branches of the economy. In a sense this is the whole point: the usual aim *is* to encourage manufacturing industry, for instance, to expand. But whether the balance may be tipped too far if one has – as is frequently the case – pressure applied from both sides with (e.g.) export taxes on agriculture and subsidies to industry is a matter for serious and constant questioning. Another point is that some concessions will tend to help small firms relatively more than big ones. This may result from the peculiar circumstances of foreign companies described above. It may also result in the accelerated depreciation case in that the value of the concession depends on the rate of interest applicable to the particular firm and this will tend to be greater for small than for large firms. The desirability of this result also calls for consideration.

[1] *Cf.* G. E. Lent, *op. cit.*, and also his 'Tax Incentives for Investment in Developing Countries', *IMF Staff Papers*, July 1967. (The latter paper is a wide-ranging review of the whole of this field.)

What the effects of these various concessions have been on
the level and composition of investment is very important but
in the nature of things very hard to discover. One of the most
searching inquiries was that by Dr A. O. Phillips in Nigeria.[1]
Some of his most important conclusions were that investment
by pioneer companies was never more than 13 % of total investment in the period investigated; out of a sample of 52 companies
only 17 mentioned tax incentives as being important in setting
up their businesses; in general, pioneer companies would have
had acceptable net profits even if there were no tax holidays;
and, perhaps most telling of all, 34 out of 94 unsuccessful appli-
cants for tax holidays still went ahead with their plans.[2]

Finally, two other ideas in this general field should receive
mention. Tax concessions are sometimes given (in various Latin
American countries, for instance) on retained profits if they are
used to purchase capital goods. This confuses two separate
issues, the encouragement to saving and the encouragement to
investment, and implies that either capital investment financed
from market funds is somehow inferior to that financed from
retained earnings or that retained earnings lent to other firms
(or the government) are inferior to retained earnings used intern-
ally on plant expenditure. Neither of these propositions strikes
one as valid under all circumstances.

The second idea was originally put forward some years ago
but has been more fully developed recently.[3] If firms are to be
subsidised, is not the right principle to make the subsidy relate

[1] A. O. Phillips, *Fiscal Incentives for Industrial Development in Nigeria* (unpublished PhD Thesis, University of Manchester, 1968). I have to thank Dr
Phillips for permission to quote his results. See also by the same author 'Nigerian
experience with Income Tax Exemptions, A Preliminary Assessment', *Nigerian
Journal of Economic and Social Studies, March* 1968.
[2] For somewhat different conclusions about the degree of success of such
policies in a Latin American country see V. Tanzi, 'Tax Incentives and Economic
Development: the Ecuadorian Experience', *Finanzarchiv*, 1969.
[3] *Cf.* A. R. Prest, *Fiscal Survey of the British Caribbean* (HMSO, 1957),
p. 102; and 'The Role of Labour Taxes and Subsidies in Promoting Employment
in Developing Countries', *International Labour Review*, April, 1971; see also J. E.
Meade, *et al.*, *The Economic and Social Structure of Mauritius* (Methuen, London,
1961), p. 24 and 'Mauritius: a case study in Malthusian Economy', *Economic
Journal* (September, 1961); also I. M. D. Little, T. Scitovsky and M. F. Scott,

to payrolls or numbers employed rather than to capital costs? At the very least this might help to correct some of the bias one often finds in favour of capital-intensive methods or industries – a bias which may be due to artificially cheap capital goods or artificially dear labour, or both. There are always difficulties both of principle (e.g. would such a scheme lead to more immigration into cities from rural areas?) and of administration (e.g. how does one prevent the number of employees being padded with relatives?). But there can surely be little doubt that, at a time when urban unemployment is one of the most menacing problems facing developing countries, this is in many ways a more satisfactory approach in principle than many of the others we have discussed. The degree of success of the plan to introduce a scheme embodying this principle in Malaysia[1] will be closely watched by many observers.

PERSONAL AND COMPANY TAX INTEGRATION

The central issues of integration are well enough known[2] and it is unnecessary to go through them here in full. Essentially, the main problem is to ensure that retained profits are not under-taxed and distributed profits are not over-taxed, given the tax rates prevailing on other forms of income. A system of taxing personal income only would, except where capital gains were taxed on an accruals (not a realisation) basis, imply exemption of undistributed profits and so would fall at the first hurdle. On the other hand, a system of taxing all corporation profits entirely independently of taxing dividends at normal personal income tax rates would fall at the second hurdle – except in the cases where corporation taxes are deemed not to rest on share-holders at all or where the need for high retention ratios is deemed paramount.

Industry and Trade in Some Developing Countries (Oxford University Press, Oxford, 1970).
[1] See *Income Tax Incentives* (*Amendments*) *Act*, Kuala Lumpur, 1971.
[2] C. S. Shoup, *Public Finance, op. cit.*, pp. 315–21 and *The Fiscal System of Venezuela* (Johns Hopkins, Baltimore, 1959), pp. 117–75.

Any method of avoiding either of these extreme situations must take account of both equity and allocation matters. Inequity can arise if dividend recipients as a whole are treated differently to others or if, even though there be no discrimination against dividend recipients as a class, there is differential treatment within that class. Inefficient allocation arises if the total or the particular uses of company saving cannot be defended (e.g. if companies with high retention rates only grow slowly). Although there are some devices which solve all these problems in principle (e.g. subjecting accruals of capital gains to the appropriate marginal rate of personal income or imputing retained profits to shareholders and subjecting such imputed income, as well as dividends paid in cash, to personal income tax) there are various practical snags associated with them. In reality, the choice of techniques is confined to two methods of partial integration; the split-rate type of company tax (whereby undistributed profits are taxed more heavily than those distributed) and the gross-up or imputation system (whereby the company pays tax at a uniform rate on all its profits, dividends to shareholders are grossed up to allow for this and a credit is given against personal income tax liability on the grossed up dividend, in respect of attributable company tax).

The choice between these two systems and the details of their application depend on several criteria. The first is what other taxes exist, other than company and personal income taxes. Obviously, the presence or absence of a capital gains tax or some form of wealth tax makes a difference in this context. Secondly, we need to know, or at least to have some rough idea of, the extent to which any tax on companies works itself through into higher prices of its products rather than lower profits. The case for integration is clearly stronger in the latter than in the former case. The third criterion is the importance of inward investment in a country. A good case can be made for the superiority of the imputation over the split rate system when there are a number of subsidiaries of foreign companies paying dividends abroad. Effectively, the split rate system may result in a lower national income to the outpaying country than the imputation system which restricts relief for company tax to domestic shareholders.[1]

Given this welter of possibilities, there can clearly be no universal guide to developing countries in such matters. Although they are all likely to be in receipt of inward investment, the possibilities of passing corporation tax forward and the case for profit retention must surely differ a good deal from one country to another.[2] So it is not surprising that we find systems varying all the way from non-integration (e.g. Kenya) to virtually complete integration (e.g. Malaysia).

[1] *Cf.* J. F. Chown, *The Reform of Corporation Tax* (Institute for Fiscal Affairs, London, 1971).

[2] R. M. Bird, *Public Finance and Economic Development* (Harvard University Press, Cambridge, Mass., 1970), p. 81, takes the view that in Colombia forward shifting is sufficiently great that one need not worry about integration problems.

3

Consumption-based Taxes

Our concern in this chapter is to assess the feasibility and desirability of financing the long term upward trend in government expenditure by various consumption-based taxes. We shall start with taxes on foreign trade, import and export taxes, and this will naturally lead to a closely allied subject, the marketing boards prominent in West Africa and elsewhere during the postwar period. Subsequently, we shall examine the role of excise taxes, various types of sales taxes and expenditure taxation.

Although there are close affinities between profits from public utilities and excise taxes, we shall postpone consideration of the former to Chapter 6, where we shall be dealing more generally with public utilities. It might be asked why expenditure taxation is discussed in this chapter rather than in the preceding one. Essentially, the answer is that we are trying to group together here most of the taxes that are based on consumption and so do not differentiate against investment and saving in the same way as a full-bodied income-tax. To be completely logical, we should include such taxes as income-taxes with 100% initial allowances (covered in Chapter 2) and payroll taxes (covered in Chapter 5).[1] But for a variety of reasons it seemed better to keep these separate. Finally, it will be obvious that this chapter owes a great deal to the recent erudite and wide-ranging survey of a large part of this field by J. F. Due.[2]

IMPORT DUTIES

The most cursory glance at UN statistics[3] shows the importance

---

[1] See C. S. Shoup, *Public Finance, op. cit.*, for the authoritative demonstration of the kinship relation between such taxes.

[2] J. F. Due, *Indirect Taxation in Developing Economies* (Johns Hopkins, Baltimore, 1970).

[3] *UN Statistical Yearbook* 1969, *op. cit.* See also J. F. Due, *op. cit.*, p. 194, for more detailed analysis.

of import duties in the finances of developing countries. Whereas eighteen developed countries were found on average to raise 7.2% of total revenue from import duties, the ratio for twenty-three developing countries was 28.2%. Among the latter we find ratios as high as 48% (Ecuador and Nigeria) whilst the lowest (Zambia 7.6%) was higher than the mean figure for developed countries. The reasons for the importance of import duties are partly historical, i.e. that imports were the basis from which the cash economy permeated a country. But there are present-day justifications too. If imports bear a large ratio to GNP, as is frequently (though not invariably) the case in these countries, it is obviously reasonable to lay taxes on them. It can also be claimed that taxing imports may be at the expense of foreigners rather than residents if the supply curve of the former is highly inelastic; or that the main burden will fall on domestic importers' quasi-rents rather than on domestic consumers if, for instance, supplies are limited by import quotas. Import duties are often imposed for protective reasons but in this case they are more successful the less revenue they yield, and so we leave this major issue aside here. Perhaps most important of all is the administrative argument – that there is a limited number of ports in a country, that goods arrive in bulk containers (ships or aircraft) which cannot easily escape detection and so on. Indeed, some observers have been so impressed by the general advantages of collecting taxes in this form in under-developed countries that they have argued for greater rather than lesser reliance on this mode of taxation.

Reliance on import duties is not always easy, however. First of all, there may be technical difficulties. The use of quota restrictions may be thought necessary in the interests of short-term balance of payments equilibrium; but the goods whose supply is judged dispensable may be the very ones which are highly productive in import duty yield – as some countries which have banned car imports have found out. Another technical complication is that many import tax structures have in the past been arranged on a specific rather than an *ad valorem* basis especially when high rates of duty were imposed and when the goods in question varied little in quality and price. To keep in step with price changes may then require special legislation every time. A different sort of point is the danger of evasion. The stories of smuggling in Britain in the old days of high duties on brandy, silk, and the like, are now part of history, but they have their modern counterparts, especially where there are long contiguous frontiers, where supply (or demand) is plentiful on the other side of the frontier and where the neighbouring governments lack the will or ability, or both, to cope with such traffic. Professor Shoup[1] has recently estimated that only about 40% of legal obligations on import duties are met in Liberia – partly due to smuggling, but also to undervaluation and mislabelling.

The more purely economic objections to extensive reliance on import duties are several. There is first the familiar clash between the need (from a long term revenue viewpoint) to tax commodities for which income elasticity of demand is high and the need to offer incentives to producers to edge further into the market economy – which means taxing less heavily those consumer goods which producers are likely to buy out of marginal cash earnings. This is common to indirect taxes other than import duties (e.g. excise duties) but it may be especially relevant in the case of import duties in so far as incentive goods are, at any rate in the early stages of growth, more likely to be imported than home-produced. Furthermore, reliance on taxing consumer goods for which there is a high income elasticity of demand will imply more than proportionate reductions in revenue when incomes fall. We shall return to this point shortly when we come to export duties. On the other hand, the concentration of import duties on goods for which there is a low income elasticity of demand is unlikely to commend itself to those with egalitarian notions of income distribution. And as far as capital goods and raw materials are concerned, it is often a matter of policy to exempt these in order to encourage the growth of domestic industry.

Further points come up if frequent changes in rates of import duties are contemplated. Resultant upward movements in

[1] *The Tax System of Liberia, op. cit.*

retail prices may help to generate demands for higher wages and it is unlikely that any inflationary consequences will be completely offset when prices fall. We also run into all the difficulties of importers, and others, holding quantities of tax-paid stocks and thus being liable to suffer capital gains and losses as tax rates vary. This is not a disastrous result but it is, to say the least, inconvenient and likely to result in loud and frequent protests to the authorities.

All in all, one would expect to find fairly heavy reliance on import duties in the early stages of development[1] but for this to diminish gradually as more and more consumer goods are produced domestically. One of the most persistent problems in such a transition is the tendency to retain protective elements of duty long after the need for them has vanished. Although this feature of commercial policy is not of primary concern in the present context, it is of such general importance that no opportunity of drawing attention to it can be missed.

EXPORT TAXES[2]

Taxation of exports,[3] although far from being a recent innovation,[4] has only become a well-known phenomenon in the postwar world. Quite apart from the multiple exchange rates in Latin American countries (which can best be described as a system of differential taxation of imports and/or exports, visible and invisible), there have been a number of other countries which have derived a substantial part of their revenue from this

[1] Note, for instance, the differing importance of such duties in total revenue in countries with GNP of less than $500 per head and those with higher figures (cf. J. F. Due, op. cit., p. 194).

[2] For a fuller discussion see R. Goode, G. E. Lent, and P. D. Ojha, 'The Role of Export Taxes in Developing Countries', *IMF Staff Papers*, November 1966.

[3] Most of the arguments about export taxation apply in the case of royalties levied on minerals, etc, at least if they relate to output or price. Where they are more nearly related to profits, the analogy with income taxation is closer. For detailed discussion see H. W. T. Pepper, 'The Fiscal Treatment of Mineral Operations', *Bulletin of International Fiscal Documentation*, September and October 1968.

[4] Export duties were imposed in Ceylon from 1803 to 1854.

type of levy. In 1969, for instance, Ghana derived 20% of its revenue from this source and Ceylon 12%.[1] This is an immense change from the pre-war situation where this sort of tax was virtually unknown. In some cases, tax rates are fixed at specific levels (£x per ton etc) but in others (e.g. Malaysia) duties have been levied on a sliding scale basis, the effective rate of duty increasing as price increases.

A number of advantages can be claimed for this form of taxation. From an administrative point of view it is even more acceptable than import duties in that the variety and complexity of goods exported and the number of firms engaged in export transactions are both likely to be less than on the import side. It is, for instance, very much easier to fix and administer a tax on cocoa exports from Ghana than on the multifarious imports into the country. There are also some more narrowly economic arguments for this form of taxation. If any individual country is in a monopolistic position in the world market, it is conceivable that the whole or a large part of the tax can be passed on to foreigners without any appreciable reduction in the volume of sales. However, too much importance cannot be attached to this point as there are very few countries in this position, even in the short run, and even fewer if one allows for the growth of competition in the long run (e.g. the classic example of Chilean nitrates). It is also sometimes argued that there are advantages to be gained from taxing all producers, whether marginal or intra-marginal, at the same rate per quantum of exports, compared with an income tax which takes the same proportion of everyone's profit. The strength of this argument depends on the relative effectiveness of reductions in net producer prices and reductions in the rate of return on capital on the outputs of different producers; but it seems doubtful whether it has any general validity. Finally it can be argued that if an export tax is imposed at a time when exporters' incomes are rising, whether through larger outputs or higher prices, or both, this may simply amount to a tax on windfall gains and in principle such taxation is acceptable and even desirable. This

[1] *UN Statistical Yearbook*, 1969.

argument is more acceptable in respect of demand than supply changes (the latter may be due to, say, weather changes but may also be the result of effort and initiative), but even in the former case it is more telling in the short than in the long run.

These arguments for export taxation can be countered in a number of ways. The first point is that export taxation discriminates (except when the tax is passed on to foreigners) between taxed and non-taxed commodities. As a consequence, the allocation of resources may be affected in three ways. First there will be a tendency for exporters of taxed commodities to divert output to the home market or to find illicit channels of export. Second, in so far as there are any export goods not subject to export taxation, there will be some shift of resources towards them. Third, in so far as export taxes cover the whole range of goods going abroad, there will be a tendency to concentrate on other lines of output destined for domestic consumption – and possibly a further tendency to retreat into the subsistence sector of the economy. These matters have been discussed a great deal in recent years[1] and so it is unnecessary to explore them further here, except to say that it is now accepted by many that the disincentive effects of export taxes are so great that undue reliance should not be placed on them as a fiscal instrument. Attacks have also been made on the equity of export duties. Although it can be argued that in the short run there is nothing very reprehensible about laying especially heavy taxes on people with especially large increases in incomes, there is clearly no justification for permanent discrimination of this sort. To argue otherwise would imply that there was some inherent reason for taxing producers of some commodities more heavily than others, and in the particular context of most underdeveloped countries, for taxing farmers more than non-farmers.

[1] E.g. P. T. Bauer and B. S. Yamey, *The Economics of Underdeveloped Countries* (Nisbet and Cambridge University Press, 1957), Ch. XIII. Also R. Nurkse, 'Trade Fluctuations and Buffer Policies of Low Income Countries', *Kyklos*, 1958. See also Goode, Lent and Ojha, *op. cit.*, p. 467 for references to findings about the (positive) elasticity of supply of primary producers. These suggest that such re-actions can only be ignored when, for instance, there is an internationally agreed quota on exports and when output is currently running above that level.

There is one further point to make here. It can be argued that as the effective levying of income taxation on farmers is so difficult, export taxation is a reasonable substitute. The snag here is that export taxation by definition only taxes output not assigned to the home market. Therefore, although one makes up for the deficiencies of income taxation in the case of some producers, others still escape the tax net. At best, therefore, export taxation is only a partial substitute for income taxation of agricultural producers.

Another point about export taxation is that in so far as the amount payable increases at a time of windfall gains in income, it is likely that the additional tax revenue is to some degree at the expense of private saving rather than consumption.[1] The desirability of public rather than private saving raises many fundamental issues beyond the scope of this chapter and so we shall do no more than offer the somewhat platitudinous observation that in so far as one wishes to encourage private saving as a means of developing such countries, this is hardly the right way to set about it.

A final point about export taxation is that its yield will fluctuate, maybe more than proportionately, with the volume of exports and conceivably with the price as well. We have referred to the volatility of exports already and so we can jump straight to the conclusion that the yield of export duties is likely to be unstable from one year to another.[2] When export taxes amount to 20–30% of total government revenue, this must in turn imply appreciable fluctuations in the total. Nor can the budgetary effects be readily defended on standard Keynesian principles when these fluctuations stem from abroad rather than at home.

In the long run, we must expect that reductions in the ratio of exports to GNP and changes in the composition of exports – from primary products to manufactures, for instance – will

[1] Some striking evidence of the high marginal propensity to save of peasant cocoa producers was given by Galletti, Baldwin and Dina, *Nigerian Cocoa Farmers* (Oxford University Press, Oxford, 1956), pp. 461–2.
[2] E.g. whereas the value of exports from Ceylon fell by 11% between 1953 and 1956, export duty receipts fell by 19%.

69

reduce the dependence on export taxes as a source of revenue. As tax administration improves and more revenue can be raised by income taxes as well as excise and sales taxes, the process will be intensified. Nevertheless, a number of countries are going to rely on raising sizeable amounts of revenue by this means for years to come.

MARKETING BOARDS

During and since the Second World War a number of countries have set up semi-official agencies which have been given statutory monopolies of export crops, with powers to fix producers' prices and, if thought fit, to accumulate reserves out of the difference between world and domestic prices or to use accumulated reserves to bolster up producer prices. Well-known examples have been the former British West African territories (Ghana, Nigeria, Sierra Leone and Gambia), but there have been others in East and Central Africa (e.g. Uganda and Malawi) and elsewhere.

It can be argued that the operations of such boards do not really come within the scope of government finance, as the financial operations of such bodies do not enter into government accounts. However, the administrative connection with government is usually very close and the degree of independence small; historically, there has been a close connection between marketing boards and export taxes, the former sometimes paving the way for the latter; finally the economic resemblance between export taxes and marketing board surpluses is close. Therefore it seems appropriate to say a little about them.

Many of the arguments about export taxation apply in the case of marketing boards. Thus it can be maintained that it is a relatively easy administrative operation to drive a wedge between export prices and producer prices; that this is a means of helping to stabilise internal prices and incomes; that it is reasonable to tax windfall gains of income heavily; but that there are severe limitations to these policies from the viewpoint of both economic efficiency and equity.

Marketing board operations may be such that their effects differ from those of export taxes. For instance, export taxes may simply be levied at a given rate per quantum for any given quality of cocoa, palm oil etc. Whether marketing board operations have the same effect will depend on whether they penetrate more deeply into the economy. If the boards purchase produce at the stage when it reaches the ports they could in principle have effects on producers exactly similar to those due to export taxes. If, on the other hand, marketing boards fix prices at buying points in the hinterland the repercussions on the pattern, organisation and location of production may be very different. This is a subject which has been very fully explored by others[1] and we need not go into it further. The reason for bringing it up was simply to show that the effects of export taxes and marketing board surpluses may differ in various respects.

A more important topic is the whole rationale of marketing board operations. A good deal has been written about this in recent years and we can only look at some aspects of it. The central question is whether a system whereby marketing boards accumulate surpluses over a long period of time can be justified. This is not a very precise formulation; 'a long period of time' can have an infinity of meanings. But it will suffice to start us off. If a marketing board has surpluses year after year these will, by and large, play the same role in the economy as a permanent system of export taxation. On the other hand, a marketing board is not usually a direct government agency and its financial operations do not enter into government accounts. If it is argued that the marketing board is set up for the benefit of the producers, its role should be akin to that of a trustee. On this basis, it may be desirable to withhold some of the crop proceeds from producers in any given year but it is quite wrong that this should be more than a temporary act. To argue otherwise would be tantamount to saying that taxation rights should be delegated by the government and this is clearly unacceptable

---

[1] Cf. P. T. Bauer, *West African Trade* (Cambridge University Press, Cambridge, 1954, Part 5), and G. K. Helleiner, *Peasant Agriculture, Government and Economic Growth in Nigeria* (Irwin, Homewood, Illinois, 1966).

as a general principle. One cannot have it both ways; if an organisation is to have taxation rights it should be integrated with the government, and if it is not to be integrated it must not act so as to be a permanent instrument of taxation of the producer groups it is supposed to represent.

If this line of argument holds, as surely it must, a further conclusion follows. The amounts of taxation imposed on producers of marketing board commodities in any given period of years are not measured precisely by the accumulated funds of a board. Quite apart from any capital gains or losses of reserve funds, any outpayments other than to producers or the marketing board administration will also represent an element of taxation on the producers concerned, even though they may be for what many think are worthy causes such as helping universities or making grants for industrial development. It seems extremely doubtful whether any such outpayments are really consistent with the notion of marketing boards as trustees.

This general principle – that if marketing boards are to be autonomous bodies they should not be instruments of permanent taxation – is easier to enunciate than to put into effect. There are both conceptual and practical difficulties in identifying 'good' and 'bad' years and, therefore, whether producers should be paid less or more than the true market price. However, even if one cannot hope for perfection in such matters, there are degrees of imperfection. It is clear from Professor Helleiner's calculations[1] that over the years 1947–62, the various marketing boards in Nigeria acted pretty consistently as agents for keeping producers' incomes below the levels potentially possible. Although the very heavy deductions of the early post-war period were subsequently modified, marketing board operations were such as to make deductions from, rather than additions to, producer incomes in the much leaner years of the later 1950s and early 1960s in three out of five cases. In no case was the reduction in potential producer income less than 7% over the period as a whole and in one case (palm kernels) it was 15%. These deductions were additional to those arising from export

[1] Helleiner, *op. cit.*, p. 163.

taxes and produce purchase taxes – the total of all deductions averaging 32% in the case of cocoa and 28% with palm kernels over the whole period.

EXCISE TAXES

Excise taxes have several distinguishing characteristics. The first is that, whatever the nominal coverage, they are best thought of as being imposed on domestic as distinct from imported sources of supply; they are the domestic counterpart of import duties imposed for revenue raising purposes. They are also highly discriminatory in character and are usually imposed on a specific rather than an *ad valorem* basis. So although they shade into other forms of consumption-based taxes, they do have sufficient character of their own to warrant separate treatment.

Taking a wide definition of excise duties,[1] one can distinguish four groups: tobacco and alcohol, petrol, services, and manufactures. The relative importance of the components varies enormously from one country to another, e.g. tobacco ranges from 0 to 71%, alcohol from 0 to 56%, and motor fuel from 0 to 98%.[2] There is also a great deal of variation in the degree of reliance on excise duties as a whole; the central government of India imposes such taxes on more than seventy different commodities and raises some 40–50% of its revenue in this way,[3] whilst in other countries (e.g. Gambia) the contribution is negligible. On the other hand, the proportion of total revenue due to excises does not seem to vary very systematically with income per head in a country; there are minor changes as countries ascend the income ladder but that is all.[4]

[1] *Cf.* Due, *op. cit.*, Ch. 3 *passim*.
[2] *Ibid*, p. 75, but note the accompanying warning: 'A failure to show revenue from a particular source may indicate that domestic production has not yet developed or that a customs duty is collected on importation of materials instead of an excise on domestic production'.
[3] For a critical appraisal see R. J. Chelliah, *Fiscal Policy in Underdeveloped Countries*, second edition (Allen and Unwin, London, 1969), pp. 181–4.
[4] Due, *op. cit.*, p. 194.

Although any full explanation of these movements, or lack of them, must obviously take account of the other ways in which tax potential grows as income grows, there are in fact a number of limitations to excise duties. The first is inherent in their nature. If excise taxes are confined to a small number of commodities, they are likely to be strongly discriminatory. Although the usual sumptuary argument can be used to justify tobacco and alcohol taxes and (less strongly) the benefits of highway provision argument to justify petrol taxes,[1] the arguments for singling out particular services (hotels, cinemas etc) or particular home-produced goods are much thinner both for reasons of equity and resource allocation. If, on the other hand, excise taxes have a wide coverage, the operation of such a system becomes clumsy and invites evasion e.g. by manipulating output from higher-taxed to lower-taxed classifications. Second, the number of situations where we have a few commodities produced by a small number of large-scale enterprises (and thus easily tapped for selective excises) and a large number of commodities produced by many small-scale enterprises (and thus not easily amenable to a wide-ranging sales tax) is not likely to be enormous. At the very least, there would be a threat of small-scale operations emerging if the excise duties were raised to high levels. This is said to be a limitation on the level of excise duties on rum in the West Indies, for instance.

The administrative limitations on excise taxation are well illustrated from Liberia.[2] It was found that beer, soft drinks, and cinemas were the only excises which were effectively collected; cement and domestically produced liquor were nominally taxed – but effectively not so because of failure to publish the necessary regulations with the legislation; there was also a jewellery tax on the statute book – but no one knew why it was not applied; and landing fees at airports were virtually uncollected.

A fair summary would seem to be that alcohol, tobacco and petrol can always be relied on under this heading, but even there

---

[1] See A. R. Prest, *Transport Economics in Developing Countries* (Weidenfeld and Nicolson, London, 1969), p. 119, for fuller discussion.
[2] C. S. Shoup *et al.*, *The Tax System of Liberia, op. cit.*, p. 130.

limitations arise. Growing domestic output of manufactures and the like will often provide a source for further tax gathering but it is by no means easy to avoid the opposing dangers of over-selectiveness and over-wide coverage.

SALES TAXES[1]

Single Stage Taxes

There is a well known clash between the economic and administrative aspects of the different types of single stage sales taxes. A uniform retail sales tax has the obvious advantages of not distorting choices between different types of consumption or between consumption and saving. It is, in fact, a very close relation of a variety of other taxes with similar characteristics – value added taxation, income tax with instantaneous writing off of capital equipment, and so on – but sharply distinguishable from the normal kind of income tax. Taxes at manufacturing and wholesale stages suffer from various disadvantages, however. A wholesale tax, for instance, makes no allowances for efficiency in retailing, as the same amount of tax will be paid per quantum of sales, irrespective of whether the retailer's margin is trimmed or swollen. It may result in distortion of the relative prices of goods with different rates of stock turn.[2] There are other disadvantages of wholesale stage taxation too: retailers must face capital gains or losses on tax-paid stocks when tax rates change and devilish complications arise when transactions are direct

[1] For a useful summary of the Far East see G. E. Lent and P. D. Ojha, 'Sales Tax in countries of the Far East', *IMF Staff Papers*, January 1969.

[2] For example, suppose that the wholesale price of both A and B is 10 units but that the retail mark-up is 100% in the first case and 50% in the second because of differing rates of stock turn. If a 50% tax is introduced at the wholesale stage and percentage mark-ups are unchanged, the retail price of A will rise from 20 units to 30 units and of B from 15 units to 22½ units. In this case, the ratio of final prices is unchanged. If, however, through convention, trade agreement etc, retailers keep the same *absolute* mark-ups as before the tax, A will now sell at 25 units and B at 20 units, thereby changing their relative prices. Such a situation would not arise with retail stage taxation as the mark-ups are included in the base to which the tax is applied. See A. R. Prest, *Reform of Purchase Tax* (Hobart Paper No. 8, Institute of Economic Affairs, London, 1963).

from manufacturers to retailers or when for other reasons no recognisable wholesale price exists.[1]

In many ways the economic disadvantage of taxes at manufacturer level are even greater than those at wholesale level. A common % rate of tax at that level may not prevent markedly different % rates at the retail stage; pyramiding can all too easily occur; and there are some extremely nasty problems in specifying appropriate taxable prices.[2]

From an administrative standpoint, the advantages of the different stages are reversed. Although there are problems of taxing small manufacturers (e.g. artisan type enterprises) these are nothing whatever compared to those of taxing at the retail stage in developing countries. There is often a complex system of retail trading with a lot of different stages and a vast number of people engaged in it – a natural state of affairs in economies with insufficient capital or other resources to provide enough employment opportunities in other sectors of the economy. The sheer weight of numbers, quite apart from illiteracy, lack of accounting knowledge etc, makes it impracticable to consider such taxation seriously over more than limited areas.[3] And if taxation is confined to limited areas (e.g. big towns or big stores) this immediately introduces a discriminatory element. Further, the unit of sale is an important point; where scent is sold by the drop and cigarettes individually or even by halves[1] the problem is even worse. When we also remember the importance of subsistence and barter in some sectors (principally foodstuffs but also firewood collection, water-drawing, cloth-making, hutbuilding) the scope for effective retail sales taxation can be seen to be even further reduced.

Wholesale stage taxation is clearly less difficult in administrative respects than retail sales taxation,[5] especially if only those

[1] *Ibid*, pp. 21–2.
[2] *Cf.* J. F. Due, *op. cit.*, pp. 85–8 for authoritative discussion.
[3] For the possibilities of self-policing of retail sales taxes by the issue of redeemable coupons to consumers, see C. S. Shoup, *Public Finance, op. cit.*, pp. 434–5.
[4] P. T. Bauer, *op. cit.*, Ch. 2.
[5] *Cf.* J. F. Due *op. cit.*, p. 106, for estimates of the respective numbers of

with fairly sizeable annual turnover are counted as wholesalers, so that tax will already have been paid on goods when they reach the host of smaller intermediaries. It may also go part of the way[1] towards taxing the lower income groups not easily reached by personal income taxation. It was for reasons of this kind that in 1959 Professor Shoup and his colleagues favoured a tax of this sort for eventual introduction in Venezuela.[2]

What has in fact been the main trend in recent years? The answer seems to turn on the area of the world on which one concentrates as there are examples of new taxes on all three bases. Thus we find that Colombia, Ghana, Uganda, and Tanzania have introduced manufacturing stage taxes; Pakistan and Honduras have incorporated elements of wholesale taxation; and the Indian States offer a prime example of retail stage taxation. Tanzania seems to have put a good deal of effort into the design of its tax, which applies at either the point of import or that of manufacture, with rates of 10%, 15% and 20%. The outstanding characteristic of the State retail taxes in India is their complexity; only four have less than six rates of tax and there are many exemptions.

Multi-Stage Taxes

The disadvantages of turnover taxes levied at every stage in the production process ('cascade' taxes) in terms of artificial inducements to vertical integration and artificial deterrents to exports are well enough known not to need repetition here. Their great advantage is that they do collect a lot of revenue – so much in fact that it is very difficult to dispense with such taxes once they become embedded in the system. Chile[3] is a good example of this: it would seem that a 20% retail sales tax or a 30% manufacturing stage tax would be needed to replace its 8% (basic rate) cascade tax. On the other hand, Malaysia experimented briefly with a low-rate cascade tax in the mid-1960s but this was

manufacturers, wholesalers and retailers in Zambia, Chile and Taiwan.
[1] Though only part of the way. Like the retail tax it will not cover subsistence output.
[2] *Loc. cit.*, Ch. XI.
[3] *Cf.* Due, *op. cit.*, pp. 118–19.

not in operation for long and so success in replacing this by a levy on imports was possible.

Following the rapidly growing acceptance of value added taxation in Western Europe, there has recently been a good deal of interest in this area in developing countries. This interest has been partly at governmental level (e.g. in various Latin American countries and in Taiwan) and partly at academic level.[1] Thus it is argued that such a tax generates a great deal of information about the working of the economic system; and that if responsibility for tax collection is split between different stages instead of being concentrated at one stage, there will be less pressure for dishonesty and speculation. Without denying these arguments, it would seem that there are overwhelming disadvantages in attempting to run such tax systems in the absence of a large cadre of reliable and knowledgeable tax administrators. The consequences of multiplying the number of collection points (not to mention those of operating multiple rates or allowing exemptions from tax) are so serious as to outweigh heavily the arguments in favour.[2]

To summarise it would seem that for many years to come single stage taxes are likely to prove more fruitful than multi-stage taxes. By and large, one would expect to see an increasing role played by retail sales taxes, and a correspondingly smaller one by manufacturing and wholesale taxes as countries develop their administrative capacities. But it may well be that there is one over-riding consideration which will outweigh any other for a long time – the tendency for consumption-based taxes to 'stick to the fingers' of tax collectors, to borrow Professor Hart's phrase.[3] It may not be a bad policy aim to concentrate on tax systems which minimise such possibilities.

EXPENDITURE TAXATION

By this we mean a tax on personal income *less* saving, i.e. the

---

[1] See e.g. C. S. Shoup *et al.*, *The Tax System of Liberia*; A. G. Hart, *op. cit.*

[2] This does not, of course, preclude such possibilities as a value added tax limited to the import and domestic manufacturing stages.

[3] *Op. cit.*, p. 878.

tax is levied in essentially the same way as an income tax but the basis is spending rather than income. As we have seen, there are grounds for arguing that a tax of this kind is better discussed in a chapter on income-based taxes, the starting point for computing tax liability being income; but, on the other hand, the economic effects of such a tax are so much more akin to general sales taxes and the like than to the usual type of income tax that the balance of advantage lies with including it here. But it must be fully understood that it does not fit snugly into either chapter.

The principle of expenditure taxation has been known for a long time[1] but for many years it was regarded as completely impracticable. But in recent years both India and Ceylon, on the basis of reports prepared for them by Professor Kaldor[2] have experimented with a tax of this sort at upper income levels and therefore it is far from being a pipedream of academic economists.

There seem to be two main arguments[3] in favour of expenditure taxation as a substitute for or complement to personal income taxation in underdeveloped countries. The first is that expenditure taxation is less of a deterrent to saving than income taxation. This is a well-known general proposition and it will suffice for the time being to say that it is intuitively obvious that if one tax hits consumption and saving, and the other only consumption, the latter will tend to push people more in the direction of saving. The argument is extended by reference to the 'obvious' facts that underdeveloped countries are always in need of more saving and that in many cases it is the upper income groups particularly who need additional inducements to save rather than spend. The second main argument in favour

[1] Cf. N. Kaldor, An Expenditure Tax (Allen and Unwin, London, 1955).
[2] Indian Tax Reform, Ministry of Finance, Delhi, India, 1956. Suggestions for a Comprehensive Reform of Direct Taxation, Sessional Paper IV, 1960, Colombo, Ceylon.
[3] For fuller treatment see A. R. Prest, 'The Expenditure Tax and Saving', Economic Journal, September 1959; and 'The Expenditure Tax and Economic Development', Public Sector and Economic Development (Instituto de Estudios Fiscales, Ministerio de Hacienda, Madrid, 1963).

of expenditure taxation in these countries is the rather para-
doxical one that such taxation requires more information from
taxpayers. If the system is such that information in respect
of one tax has to tie in with that for another, it is arguable that
it will thereby become possible to check tax evasion much more
efficiently than before. An interlocking statement, it is claimed,
will enable the authorities to check inconsistencies much more
easily and thoroughly than if one simply has the usual sort of
income tax forms and returns.

Such are the arguments[1] for levying taxation in this form on
upper income groups in these countries.[2] How sound are they?
The proposition that, if an expenditure tax is substituted for an
income tax, a larger proportion of any given income is likely to
be saved is well known, the substitution effects working in
favour of more saving and the redistribution of net incomes
perhaps doing the same. If an expenditure tax is levied in addition to existing taxes, the substitution effects will normally be
nil and the income effects will tend to reduce private saving;
the increase in total saving will equal the increase in public
saving less the decrease in private saving. In the case of the relative effects of an equal yield income tax and expenditure tax, the
proviso 'of any given income' should be noted. If an expenditure
tax affects incentives to work and to take risks in such a way as
to reduce the total of income, the fact that a higher proportion
of income is saved than before will not suffice to ensure a higher
absolute level of saving. On the other hand, it will normally be
the case that an expenditure tax system imposed for a limited
period (e.g. a war emergency or a five-year development programme) will have greater savings incentives than permanent
taxes of this sort. However, these matters are very complex and
the reader is referred to the two sources mentioned for fuller
discussion.[3] Suffice it to say at this stage that the notion that

[1] There are other criteria for judging between income and expenditure taxes
(e.g. equity), but they do not seem to have more relevance to underdeveloped
than to other countries.
[2] No one seems to have proposed expenditure taxation on a mass basis in such
countries and so we do not consider this possibility here.
[3] It should be noted that all these arguments about the relative effects of

there is a large amount of luxurious consumption expenditure in these countries which can be curtailed by very simple tax legislation, thereby releasing vast sums of money for domestic capital purposes, is singularly superficial.

Another point arises in connection with upper income group saving. Any tendency for this to increase relatively to saving by others will tend to increase the concentration of private capital. How desirable this may be is a matter of opinion. The suggestion is sometimes ma dethat one can counter any such concentration by levying personal property taxes, or perhaps more highly graduated property taxes, but this is not likely to be a painless process, as the extra property taxes must themselves have some adverse effects on saving by reducing net incomes from capital and hence altering the relative attractiveness of consumption and saving at the margin.

We shall discuss problems of tax administration more fully in Chapter 7 and so one or two remarks will be sufficient for the time being. One would have thought *a priori* that an expenditure tax must encounter greater difficulties as in this case one has to measure both income and saving[1] and not just income. It is fair to make the point, as for instance Professor Kaldor did in his *Indian Tax Reform*, that the usual rough and ready assessments of income are far from satisfactory and a more refined definition of that concept would incur much heavier administrative expenses. However, this simply points to the complications of a better defined income tax; it does nothing to mitigate the fact that the administrative costs of an expenditure tax are bound to be heavy. The proposition that administration will be much easier if every individual concerned can be made to submit a balance sheet is a nice point in logic; but one's mind boggles at some of the practical implications. Even such harmless-looking notions as spreading durable goods expenditures over five- or ten-year periods run into all sorts of practical difficulties.

income and expenditure taxes on saving apply, *mutatis mutandis*, to any comparison between income taxes and indirect taxes on consumer goods.

[1] E.g. ought saving to include expenditure on buying and maintaining race-horses, as was allowed in the Indian legislation?

The history of the expenditure tax experiments in India and Ceylon does little to remove these doubts. In India the tax was originally imposed in 1958 but it has had a chequered history since then, having been taken off at one stage, restored and then taken off again. It never applied to more than a very small number of people and was totally insignificant as a means of raising revenue – the sums collected being far less than originally estimated.[1] The history of the tax in Ceylon is just as offputting; it started in 1959/60 with great expectations but the paucity of revenue yield and the plentitude of staff needed to operate it quickly forced abandonment.

It could be argued that these experiences are not decisive as in both countries the tax was used as a device for clapping on additional burdens at higher income levels rather than as a substitute for income taxation. It could not be expected that the simultaneous imposition of income tax, expenditure tax, and wealth tax would generate more personal saving. There may well be something in this argument; but, nevertheless, it is hardly one which the expenditure tax progenitors in either of these countries can make.

[1] *Cf.* R. J. Chelliah, *Fiscal Policy in Underdeveloped Countries, op. cit.,* pp. 172–4, for an account of Indian experience and for the view that the major cause of failure was the difficulty of administration e.g. in distinguishing personal from business consumption.

4
Capital-based Taxes

GENERAL DISCUSSION

Capital-based taxes take several forms. The first distinction is between those which are levied on all capital assets, subject to a number of specified exemptions, and those levied on particular assets such as real estate. Normally, one would expect the former to be on a net basis, allowing for debts as well as assets; whereas the latter will be on a gross basis, as otherwise one is inviting tax avoidance by the simple device of attaching as many debts as possible to the particular asset which is subject to tax. A second distinction is between taxes on wealth which are levied on a recurrent basis (e.g. a net wealth tax or a property tax) and those which are (purportedly, at least) on a once-for-all basis, such as a capital levy at the end of a war. A third distinction is between taxes on wealth, whether measured on a gross or a net basis, and taxes on wealth transfers. The latter may in turn be confined to transfers taking place at death or may also relate to *inter-vivos* transfers as well. Finally, we have taxes on increments in capital value, though these can claim an alternative place in a chapter on income-based taxes, as we have already seen.

Powerful arguments can be advanced for allotting places to these various taxes in a rationally ordered tax system.[1] A general tax on net wealth can be justified both in terms of economic efficiency and equity. The economic efficiency arguments relate to the exemption of human capital and better deployment of physical capital in the context of a net wealth tax, compared to an income tax. Given the usual income tax pattern, one would normally expect a net wealth tax to be more conducive to risk-taking, essentially on the grounds that an income tax is based

---

[1] *Cf.* A. R. Prest, *Public Finance in Theory and Practice*, fourth edition (Weidenfeld and Nicolson, London, 1970), Ch. XV, for fuller discussion.

83

on cash income only and so does not impinge on the security derived from safer types of investment, though there are some well-known qualifications to this general principle.[1] The equity arguments centre on the inadequacy of income, as normally measured for tax purposes, as the sole criterion of ability to pay; many would argue that a combination of income and capital is a much better base for measuring an individual's taxable capacity than either taken singly. Finally, it can also be argued, though perhaps with less force, than a capital tax will have some administrative benefits, in the sense of reducing the administrative costs of assessing income taxes, especially in respect of the better-off sections of the community.

There are equally well-known arguments in terms of both equity and efficiency in favour of capital levies on a once-for-all basis,[2] though usually these are in the context of some major cataclysm and so cannot be thought of as a very regular means of raising revenue.[3]

Nor does it involve a great effort to find ways of justifying taxes on capital transfers. Taxes at death can be argued for on the grounds that the announcement effects, to use Pigou's terminology, are much less than with many other taxes based on current income or expenditure, and that the right to inherit wealth down the generations is much less self-evident than that to retain possession of one's capital or income in one's own lifetime. And once the case for duties of some sort at death is admitted, that for gifts *inter-vivos* follows very closely behind. This can be argued for in terms of general principle: if there is a strong case for taxes on transfers at death there is also some case for taxes on transfers in life. And if the appeal to general principle is found unconvincing, that of expediency remains, i.e., that some sort of gifts tax arrangement (even if only to cover, say, the five years before death) must be made, if taxes at death are to have any significance at all.

[1] *Ibid.*, p. 43 ff.
[2] *Cf.* J. R. Hicks, U. K. Hicks and L. Rostas, *The Taxation of War Wealth* (Oxford University Press, 1942), for a definitive study.
[3] The levy imposed in Ceylon in 1970 could hardly be repeated in view of the punitive rates involved (25% on assessable capital exceeding Rs. 800,000).

The general arguments about capital gains taxation have been touched on in Chapter 2 and so we need not repeat them here, beyond saying that for an income tax to be anything like comprehensive in its coverage, one simply has to grasp this nettle, whether by the bare (iron) hand or the velvet-gloved one.

One final proposition about the case for capital taxes; it is a mistake to think that one brand is a simple substitute for another. Thus, even if one had a comprehensive net wealth tax, there would still be arguments of principle for taxing transfers of capital wealth and for taxing capital gains. It may be possible to devise a tax scheme which fulfils more than one of the functions, e.g., some people[1] have propounded the idea of a capital receipts tax which, *inter alia*, would encompass inheritances as well as capital gains. However this may be, it is important to understand that the objectives of taxing the *stock* of capital, *accretions* in value of the stock and *transfers* of the stock are separate and that success in achieving one such objective is not an excuse for passivity or inaction with respect to the others.

Despite the apparent strength of these arguments of general principle, the fact remains that so far developing countries have not been conspicuously successful in levying taxes of this kind. We saw in Chapter 1 (page 25) that the degree of reliance on these members of the tax family has not been all that great. More details have been assembled in a convenient form by Tanabe[2] who shows, for instance, that the net wealth taxes imposed in recent years in India, Pakistan and Ceylon only had a revenue yield of something between 1 and 2% of total national revenue. The particular details of the legislation are obviously a partial explanation (e.g., the very high exemption levels when expressed as a fraction of per capita income[3]), but it would also seem likely that there are some more general reasons why one should not pitch one's hopes too high for such taxes or their near relatives. First and foremost, there are the manifold problems of

[1] *Cf.* C. T. Sandford, *Realistic Tax Reform* (Chatto and Windus, London, 1971), Ch. 7.

[2] N. Tanabe, 'The Taxation of Net Wealth', *IMF Staff Papers*, March 1967, p. 142.

[3] *Ibid*, p. 137.

administration. Quite apart from the well-known accounts of inexperienced or corrupt tax inspectors we have the simple point that general capital taxes are far easier to impose, assess and levy when a lot of assets are held in the form of publicly quoted shares in large companies. When small businesses taking a non-incorporated form or without public quotation are the rule, the complications are hideously and infinitely worse. And even if, by some unimaginable miracle, these difficulties could be put on one side, it could reasonably be argued that the case in principle for general taxes on the holding or transfer of capital assets is less compelling than in more advanced countries. This is partly that arguments in terms of equity – a major prop for capital taxation – are of less importance in developing countries than in more advanced ones. It is also the case that although taxes on capital may have advantages over income taxes in securing a better disposition of the available stock of capital resources, they may also act as a deterrent to the enlargement of that stock. A general income tax has well-known disadvantageous effects on saving and/or investment relative to the usual value added tax or consumption tax; an income tax combined with a capital tax will multiply these disadvantages.[1]

All in all, it would seem that for some time to come much the most promising 'tax-handle' in this group of taxes is likely to be real estate taxation. The relative importance of other types of capital is much less in developing than in advanced countries and so by this means one is in effect taxing an important part of the stock of capital assets, despite the restriction in scope. Furthermore, there is a long and ancient history of land taxation in many countries;[2] this forms a far better base for administrative codes and practices than can be obtained for other types of

[1] Cf. C. S. Shoup, *Public Finance*, Chs. 9 and 14 for the argument in full.
[2] E.g. Lugard found a system of land tax in existence in Northern Nigeria when he took over the area in the early 1900s. India provides other examples of land taxes established many years ago and traditionally of great importance – thus Keynes wrote in 1909: 'About 40% of the net revenue of the country is derived from land revenue, the most economical and least oppressive of all forms of taxation' (Royal Economic Society, *The Collected Writings of John Maynard Keynes*, Vol. XV, Macmillan, London, 1971, p. 38).

capital assets. There has also been a great deal of study of land and cognate taxes in recent years. Accordingly, we shall confine ourselves to the subject of real estate taxes for the rest of this chapter – essentially on the grounds that for some time to come this is likely to be the real part of the capital area where taxation can be important in developing countries, though without prejudice to other developments which may be possible in the more distant future.

REAL ESTATE TAXATION

Turning to taxation of land and real estate, we have to distinguish between three different types of taxes – those on capital values, those on increments in capital values due to general causes and those on increments associated with very specific changes.[1] And in all three cases we may be taxing land itself, or the improvements made to it, or a mixture of the two.

Taxes on Capital Values

Taxation of land values can take a large number of different forms and so it is important to classify them. The first distinction is between *unimproved*, *site* and *improved* values. Unimproved values can be thought of as the 'original and indestructible power of the soil', to use Ricardo's phraseology; site values include such expenses as may have been incurred in levelling or draining land; and improved values include the additions due to building or construction of any kind. We shall not be concerned here with unimproved values; land tax planners do not usually concern themselves with anything less than the site value concept. But we shall need to say quite a lot about the relative merits of the site and improved value bases. We may note in passing that improvements due to better use of fertilisers and the like are normally counted as part of site values; it is essentially the element of building or construction which is the basis of the distinction.

[1] *Cf.* G. E. Lent, 'The Taxation of Land Value', *IMF Staff Papers*, March 1967, for an authoritative general review. H. P. Wald, *Taxation of Agricultural Land in Underdeveloped Economies* (Harvard University Press, Cambridge, Mass., 1959) remains the standard work. See also *UN Manual of Land Tax Administration* (UN, New York, 1968).

A second line to be drawn is that between taxes on urban and rural real estate. We frequently find taxes levied in urban but not in rural areas; and even when taxes are levied in both, they may be on a different basis (e.g., improved values in urban areas; site values in rural) or authorised by different laws or levels of government. However, this distinction is more one of practical usage than of economic logic.

Next comes the basis for calculating capital values. Wald[1] lists an almost bewildering variety of land taxes in different countries and levied on different bases. Capital values may be derived directly from sales prices or by capitalising annual values; and the latter may be approximated by the use of turnover or output data. Cruder forms of taxation based on land area are also to be found; and so are more sophisticated ones based on potential rather than actual output. Finally, tax rates may be on a proportional or a progressive basis; this choice has some important consequences.

Arguments for Land Taxation

A general justification for land taxation can be found in the usual arguments for capital taxes as set out above, i.e., advantages for risk-taking, equity and so on. More particular reasons exist for the emphasis often accorded to land taxes. These are sometimes of a historical character, e.g., the example of the Japanese use of land taxation in the latter part of the nineteenth century has often been quoted with approval,[2] Another reason for emphasising land taxes is the simple one that the ratio of reproducible fixed capital to land is smaller than would be found in economically advanced countries and therefore the major weight of capital taxation must inevitably fall on land. More purely analytical arguments are of several kinds.

First, we have the efficiency aspect. Whereas taxes on land improvements must be expected to have substitution effects

---

[1] *Op. cit.*

[2] *Cf.* R. Nurkse, *Problems of Capital Formation in Underdeveloped Countries* (Blackwell, Oxford, 1953); R. P. Sinha, 'Unresolved Issues in Japan's Early Economic Development', *Scottish Journal of Political Economy*, June 1969, for the view that the importance of land taxation in Japan has been exaggerated.

as well as income effects, thereby discouraging investment in this form, taxes on land as such can be so arranged as to have income effects only. Similarly, it can be argued that land is an asset which cannot migrate, in sharp contrast (whatever the law may say) to many forms of financial investment. The precise size of the income effects on landowners will obviously depend on the precise comparison being made – which other taxes (expenditures) would fall (rise) if a land tax were exacted and whether land-owners would be affected by these concomitant income effects – but the general principle is clear enough.

The next proposition is that any such land tax will induce landowners to utilise their land more intensively, whether by bringing wholly idle land into use or by fuller cultivation of land already in use. This is particularly important when some land remains entirely idle, whilst other land supports a large number of people. Thus, for instance, Furtado[1] has shown that in Chile in the mid-1960s the value of output per hectare of land *owned* was for the *latifundios* (larger estates) only 5% of that for the *minifundios* (small holdings); whereas it was 21% in respect of land *cultivated*. This implies that the proportion of cultivated to total land in *latifundios* conditions was only about one quarter of that found under *minifundios* conditions. Although the current differences in output per worker in the two types of farming[2] would presumably be reduced if the tax were such that there were more extensive cultivation in one case and less intensive cultivation in the other, it would seem reasonable to suppose that extra output would be forthcoming in these circumstances.

Many argue that a land tax could have desirable equity, as well as efficiency consequences. If it were sufficiently heavy in the case of large owners for them to be forced to sell some of their land, this would lead to a more equal distribution of wealth between rich and poor, or at the very least it would slow down the movement towards more unequal distribution. Whilst

[1] C. Furtado, *The Economic Development of Latin America* (Cambridge University Press, Cambridge, 1970), p. 52.
[2] Value of output per agricultural worker was some four times higher in *latifundios* (*ibid.*).

noting that the precise character of such effects must depend on the revenue and/or expenditure alternatives, one further argument does need comment. Large scale agriculture tends to be associated with more capital intensive methods and so land redistribution might be expected to be more favourable to labour intensive methods and to greater employment opportunities. However, one might very well find that any such extra agricultural employment was at the expense of agricultural output; if so, a complex assessment of all the resultant benefits and costs would be needed.

It can also be argued that the rural sector as a whole is under-taxed relatively to urban areas in some countries. This, however, is a much weaker argument than the others. First, it is unlikely to hold in countries raising substantial sums by export duties or similar devices; and second, even if it does hold it does not follow that additional taxation should necessarily take the form of a tax on land. Another proposition, grossly fallacious, should also be mentioned – that land taxes need to be levied to prevent too large a proportion of total savings going into land-holding. It is, of course, impossible for savings to be used up in the purchase of an *existing* asset, whether it be land, property, gold, jewellery or anything else of that nature; the purchase of an existing asset immediately releases the vendor's capital for employment elsewhere.

Problems with Traditional Land Taxes
Despite these advantages, taxes on land rarely play a major part in the finances of developing countries, as the work of both Wald and Lent shows.[1] There seem to be several reasons for this state of affairs. The first is that there are formidable problems of implementing taxes on land. For a start, one has to have a clearly defined pattern of land ownership. In some African countries, there are only individual rights to cultivate rather than to own land; in others, land ownership is inordinately

[1] *Op. cit.* See also Organisation of American States, *Fiscal Survey of Panama* (Johns Hopkins, Baltimore, 1964), Ch. 4 for an account of the difficulties encountered with land taxation in that country.

fragmented, even to the extent of the division of single trees among several owners. Clearly, the intricacy of this problem varies from one country to another;[1] it is likely to be far easier where one has large estates than where one has a large element of peasant proprietorship. But even if one can sort out the pattern of ownership one then has to face all the problems of assessment, whether by reference to capital value, gross annual value or some other variant. If one tries to side-step problems of valuation by taxing at a constant rate per acre, irrespective of fertility and productivity, one is then driven to fixing a rate which the poorest land can pay – with the result that total yield is unlikely to be large. In these circumstances, re-assessment of the extent or value of ownership tend to be infrequent. Unless it is possible to alter the tax base quickly, the real value of tax receipts from this source is likely to fall over time in so far as the general price level rises. Finally, even if these more technical obstacles to land taxation can be overcome, the political power of the land-owning classes may be so strong as to prevent the introduction or effective implementation of appropriate legislation.

For these various reasons, land taxes frequently have little bite in them; but problems also arise in the contrary case where they do bite. The base for taxation may be such that improvements do not escape entirely, with consequential disincentive effects. Through the usual capitalisation process the income effects will fall entirely on those who happen to own land at the time a tax is increased or reduced. The precise extent of the windfall loss or gain will depend on the tax rate and on the prevailing discount rate;[2] but the experience of substituting site value for improved value rating in Jamaica in recent years shows that these impositions and reliefs can be very substantial.[3] Thus

---

[1] *Cf.* Lord Hailey, *An African Survey* (Oxford University Press, Oxford, 1957 edition), p. 679, for an interesting comparison between Indian and Africa in this regard.

[2] If V = sales value of land after the tax is imposed, F = sales value if no tax, i = discount rate and t = tax rate, then it follows that $\dfrac{V}{F} = \dfrac{i}{(i + t)}$ (*cf.* Colin Clark, *Population Growth and Land Use* (Macmillan, London, 1967), p. 383).

[3] Lent, *op. cit.*

we seem to have a Morton's Fork sort of situation, i.e. one where it is difficult to make a land tax work but where it produces unwelcome consequences when it does work.[1]

New Ideas in Land Taxation

There have been a number of attempts to remedy this situation in recent years, especially in Latin America. A number of countries have enacted new land taxes, some of them with very interesting features: in Guatemala and Honduras the rate of tax is greater, the longer the time during which land has been idle; and in Nicaragua it varies according to land fertility. A good deal of attention has also been given to much more far-reaching proposals.

One[2] is that land should be graded according to fertility and an initial valuation be determined on the basis of potential output; the figure for any particular plot would be kept up to date in the years between valuations by reference to an index of changes in the value of net output per acre for all agricultural land in a country; and a progressive tax rate would be applied to land values assessed in this way. An alternative would be a system of self-assessment.[3] On this scheme, the authorities would announce rough and ready valuations; if dissatisfied, landowners could opt to submit their own valuation; this would be announced publicly and the state would then have the right to buy at this price and anyone else at not less than, say, 110% of it; the owner would then have the choice of accepting an offer, or of paying tax on the basis of the offer bid or of asking for another state valuation, but at his expense; offers from private buyers would have to be accompanied by deposits but there should also

[1] For accounts of experiences in different countries see A. O. Hirschman 'Land Taxes and Land Reform in Colombia', in R. M. Bird and O. Oldman *Readings in Taxation in Developing Countries* (Johns Hopkins, Baltimore, 1967); and C. T. Edwards, *Public Finances in Malaya and Singapore, op. cit.*, pp. 329–43.

[2] *Cf.* Organisation of American States (Joint Tax Program) *Fiscal Policy for Economic Growth in Latin America* (Johns Hopkins Press, Baltimore, 1965), Ch. 10.

[3] *Cf.* J. Strasma, 'Market-Enforced Self-Assessment for Real Estate Taxation', *Bulletin of International Fiscal Documentation*, 1965, pp. 353 and 397.

be some compensation for time and effort expended by such people if their offers were rejected.

Devices of this kind would certainly meet or by-pass some of the standard difficulties of land taxation. Reference to potential, rather than actual output avoids substitution effects; self-assessment and/or annual revision of values in accordance with a general index of the value of agricultural output gets over the problems of out of date valuations. It might reasonably be claimed that more effective land taxation on these lines would make a real contribution to more effective taxation of agricultural incomes. There are possible drawbacks, however. Insistence on a progressive tax structure means that one would have to assess tax on a family rather than an individual basis, to prevent wholesale avoidance; and this would obviously be a more difficult administrative operation. Progressive tax structures would also mean that the tax could hardly be a local one, assuming that holdings would often be dispersed geographically; but a land tax – or, more generally, any kind of property taxation – is eminently suitable as a local tax in that the division of the spoils between the various authorities is so much more clear-cut than with many other taxes. Imputed changes in value over time could also cause hardships in so far as there are sharp changes in relative prices and values of different crops and hence in capital values of the corresponding land areas. The self-assessment system also has its danger; people in the know about future developments might have advantages over others, there might be collusion possibilities if the number of large land-owners were small, a system of compensation to frustrated buyers might easily degenerate into an informer system and so on.[1]

So although one must agree that ideas on these lines are full of ingenuity, one may still have reservations about whether these modern versions of land taxation will be all that much more successful than earlier ones in increasing the area of land under cultivation or in imposing taxes on unearned increments. It

[1] It is too early as yet to judge the effectiveness of the self-assessment provisions of the real property tax imposed in Peru under Decree 287 of 9 August 1968.

might well be that one should approach the whole problem some- what differently. The first question to answer is why land is held idle rather than cultivated. No doubt reasons of a sentimental or social character are part of the explanation. But in so far as economics can provide answers at all, it must surely be that people prefer non-money income yielding assets of this kind to assets which can offer a money income, because of the greater possibility of capital gains in the land case. This is no doubt a reflection of inflation psychology – the belief that land prices will rise more than those of other assets; but may it not also be that people are much more apprehensive about the security and inviolability of wealth held in other forms? If this be so, a more promising way of freeing under-utilised land might be to remove some of the restrictions or tax burdens on other assets rather than levy a swinging tax on landowners. But, of course,in those countries where landowners have paramount political power it may be just as unrealistic to expect restrictions or burdens on non-agricultural assets to be reduced as to expect land taxes to be introduced or administered with any firmness of purpose.

Taxes on General Increments in Land Values

We are concerned at this stage with increments in value arising from general causes. These may be due to the growth of popula- tion and reproducible capital; with a given land area this will tend to force up land prices, as any city dweller knows. Addition- al reasons for increments in value would be a general fall in the value of money or reductions in interest rates. We need to distinguish these various cases very sharply from that where land values rise because of some specific improvement affecting some specific area of land.

The general arguments for taxing capital gains of any kind are well-known and we need not rehearse them here.[1] The questions we have to ask are whether there is any case for exempting land, in whole or in part, if there is a general system

[1] Cf. A. R. Prest, *Public Finance in Theory and Practice* (fourth edition, Weidenfeld and Nicolson, London, 1970), Ch. XIV.

of capital gains taxation; and whether land is such a special case as to need separate treatment from all other types of capital assets.

The answer to the first question is clear-cut in principle. As J. S. Mill put it.[1]

> The ordinary progress of a society which increases in wealth is at all times tending to augment the incomes of landlords; to give them both a greater amount and a greater proportion of the wealth of the community, independently of any trouble or outlay incurred by themselves. They grow richer, as it were in their sleep, without working, risking or economising. What claim have they on the general principle of social justice, to this accession of riches?

In short, there are no convincing reasons why landowners should be exempted from any general system of capital gains taxation, especially in countries where land is so important relatively to reproducible physical capital.

The second question has several somewhat different aspects: one is whether land gains should be taxed when others are not; or whether they should be taxed at higher rates; or whether they should be taxed at the same rates but under special legislation. We shall concentrate primarily on the second case; the first can be regarded as a special case of the second and we shall try to take account of the third where relevant and necessary.

Arguments for taxing land gains at higher rates are not very convincing. One is that capital gains on land are often due to the granting of planning permission for development; thus, for instance, the UK White Paper announcing the intention to impose a betterment levy on land declared:[2] '. . . it is generally accepted that the value attached to land by the right to develop it is a value which has substantially been created by the community.'

Quite apart from criticising the fuzzy language in such a proposition ('created by the community' should read 'due to government legislation'), it is difficult to see why some acts of

[1] *Principles of Political Economy* (Ashley edition 1909), p. 818.
[2] *The Land Commission* (Cmnd. 2771, HMSO, London, September 1965).

government leading to capital gains should be put into a different category from others, e.g. those concerned with devaluation or import restrictions. Nor, for that matter, is it self-evident that the total of capital gains arising annually under a system of planning permission would differ from that arising from the operation of free markets in land, though, of course, the distribution between individual owners would in all probability differ.

Another fallacy is that land capital gains need to be taxed because other people may suffer from associated developments, e.g. loss of amenity. External effects of this sort are not the sole prerogative of land development and it would be somewhat invidious to tax them in this context only. Moreover, there is no reason for supposing that there is any simple relation between gains in capital value and the valuation of any such damages; and if taxes were justifiable on these grounds, one would also have to explain why the proceeds were not paid to the affected parties rather than amalgamated with general government revenue. An argument with rather more substance is that a special system of land gains taxation can attempt to catch capital gains as they accrue rather than when they are realised. But such ambitions are more easily stated than achieved, as the history of attempts to tax land gains shows.

The UK has now made four separate attempts – in 1909, 1931, 1947 and 1967 – to tax land capital gains by special legislation; and all four have had to be abandoned. We cannot go into this history in detail here but the main reasons for termination seem to have been the administrative complexities of operating the legislation, the failure to collect more than a very modest revenue (e.g. in 1969/70, the yield of UK betterment levy, net of administrative costs and consequential losses of revenue from other taxes, was only about £2.5m, far less than had been originally forecast)[1] and the failure to achieve some of the declared objectives of the legislation (e.g. the 1967 legislation would appear to have reduced the availability of land for

[1] Cf. D. R. Denman, 'Lessons from the Land Commission', *Three Banks Review*, March 1971.

development and thus forced up prices, rather than leaving the burden of the tax on landowners).

There is a long history of attempts to tax land gains in other countries, either on a realisation or an accruals basis.[1] But, by and large, the degree of success seems to have been very limited, both in terms of revenue yield and ease of administration.

If attempts to tax land gains at special rates or in special ways run into such difficulties, one has to ask about preferable alternatives. If a general capital gains tax is a practicable proposition, it would seem best to subsume land gains taxation under this heading, as was done in the UK in 1971. But two possible other alternatives should be noted. One is to levy a tax, such as a stamp duty, on land sales. However, this requires a system of registering land transactions; and a tax on transactions is an entirely different economic animal from one on capital gains.[2] Another alternative is that instead of trying to tax a landowner on increments in value associated with permission to develop land, all such planning permission rights should be put up to public auction; if someone other than the landowner acquires them, he would then negotiate with the latter for the sale of the land.[3] This idea has a great deal to recommend it; but whether many developing countries have the capacity to administer it as yet is another matter.

Taxes on Specific Increments in Land Values

The idea of charging landowners for the benefits derived by them from public sector decisions or actions is an ancient one.[4] Betterment charges of this kind were levied in England as long ago as 1250 when a sea-wall in Romney Marsh was repaired. The converse notion of 'worsement' was also recognised in medieval times when the four northern counties of England were

[1] G. E. Lent, *op. cit.*
[2] *Cf.* C. S. Shoup, *Public Finance, op. cit.*, p. 404; also C. Kennedy, 'Stamp Duties as a Capital Gains Tax', *Review of Economic Studies*, 1956, and C. S. Shoup, 'Comment', *ibid.*, October 1957.
[3] *Cf.* F. G. Pennance, *Housing, Town Planning and the Land Commission*, Hobart Paper 40, Institute of Economic Affairs, London 1967.
[4] *Cf.* W. Phillips, 'Betterment Taxes', *British Tax Review*, May–June 1966.

granted tax relief to compensate for cattle thefts by marauding bands of Scots. And despite the attempt by a Duke of Argyll to decry betterment as a notion which was 'absurd, foreign and vulgar', there have been many charges on these lines in more modern times. Thus street widening or improvement charges have frequently been levied on adjoining property owners in both the UK and the USA.[1] And it has long been a practice in India to levy charges on landlords and farmers in respect of benefits from irrigation schemes; Mysore levied such charges as far back as 1888.

Taxation of capital gains arising in this way is a very different kettle of fish from the gains taxation discussed earlier. Then it was primarily a matter of ability to pay or unfairness to others in not levying taxes on that sort of income; now it is a case of benefit taxation, of particular people benefitting from particular expenditures of public authorities. This leads to the first of the major problems associated with this form of taxation: the measurement of the *benefits* arising from street improvements and the like rather than their *cost*. This is obviously a more difficult operation (e.g. benefits are likely to be spread over a period of years whereas the bulk of the costs may well be incurred at the same time; and there are many tasty traps such as the distinction between *total* and *marginal* benefits and possible double counting of benefits) but the techniques of cost-benefit analysis may be of some help.[2] Even when benefits can be readily estimated in aggregate, one still has to allocate them: first, between those which can be apportioned to individuals and those which are diffused through the community at large and second, between each and every individual in the former category. There are many devices for making such allocations[3] but most of them are of a rule of thumb rather than a scientific character and also relate to cost rather than benefit apportionment. Finally, charges for such benefits are not likely to have

[1] *Cf.* G. E. Lent, *op. cit.*
[2] *Cf.* A. R. Prest and R. Turvey, 'Cost-Benefit Analysis: a Survey', *Economic Journal*, December 1965.
[3] *Cf.* G. E. Lent, *op. cit.*

the same time pattern as the costs incurred; even though there may be some degree of offsetting by matching charges for one scheme against costs for another, periodic borrowing is likely to be an inevitable feature of such arrangements, with consequential needs for debt amortisation and servicing.

5

Other Revenue Sources

To cover this subject exhaustively would be quite beyond our scope. Quite apart from all the forms of taxation not covered in Chapters 2 to 4, we should have to consider public enterprise receipts, internal borrowing (whether from the central bank or more generally), foreign borrowing (from commercial sources as well as foreign governments and international agencies) and aid of all types from abroad. In a really full treatment, one would need to think of even more indirect means of raising revenue, e.g. the promotion of international arrangements which increase the value of sales of particular exports (for instance, oil, minerals, foodstuffs), and thus facilitate revenue-raising by export taxes and the like.

In fact we shall confine ourselves to a very limited range of topics – payroll taxes, compulsory lending schemes and revenue from government lotteries and betting taxes. This is partly because these particular sources of finance have interesting and important characteristics; partly because they are well documented and it is possible to discuss them in the light of the experience of a wide range of countries.

Some details of this chapter and the following one may be noted now. We shall cover both general payroll taxes and employer contributions to social security schemes as well as other types of compulsory lending. In Chapter 6, when we come to government expenditure, we shall have something to say about the general principles of social security schemes as well as expenditure under that heading. So by this means we hope to cover all the most important aspects of this topic, emphasising the links to analogous forms of revenue, as well as the special nature of such schemes.[1] As for public enterprise, there is clearly

[1] It will be noticed that employer and employee contributions are discussed in different sections of this chapter, a procedure which might be thought to conflict

a case for saying something about it in a revenue chapter. But there are important considerations to be emphasised on the expenditure side and as, in practice, the revenue contributions are often very small, if not negative, it seemed best to take the whole of this subject under the expenditure heading of Chapter 6.

The omission of all types of voluntary lending to governments and of foreign aid from our discussion should not be taken as a sign that their importance is unrecognised. Quite the contrary. It is precisely because we now find much more complex and diverse monetary and banking systems than in the days when colonies operated on standard Currency Board systems[1] that monetary and debt policy must be regarded as a specialist subject which cannot be fitted into the compass of a new edition of this book. And international borrowing and receipts from aid have become the subject of much specialist literature[2] in recent years which it would be both impossible and superfluous to discuss here. It is also probably true to say that the extent to which economic principles are involved in requesting aid is a good deal less than in the granting of aid – and it is the former, not the latter, which is more relevant to the theme of this book.

PAYROLL TAXES

Taxes on employers' payrolls are to be found in many developing countries. A comprehensive survey of social security contributions was made in 1967 by F. Reviglio[3] and although the

with the general theoretical proposition that it is of no importance whether a tax is placed on the buyers' or sellers' side in a market, be it a market for goods or labour. The explanation is that whereas employee contributions can be thought of as a particular kind of compulsory lending, the linkage between employer contributions and any repayments is much more indirect; also there is a close affinity between all payroll taxes whether for social security or general purposes.

[1] *Cf.* the first edition of this book (Weidenfeld and Nicolson, London, 1962), Ch. 5 for an account of the way such systems operated.

[2] *Cf.* I. M. D. Little and J. M. Clifford, *International Aid* (Allen and Unwin, London, 1965); also J. M. Healey, *The Economics of Aid* (Routledge, London, 1971).

[3] F. Reviglio, 'Social Security: a Means of Savings Mobilisation for Economic Development', and 'The Social Security Sector and Its Financing in Developing Countries', *IMF Staff Papers*, July and November 1967.

details are no doubt out of date now, the general impression is likely to remain correct. The mean figure for employers' contributions in forty-six developing countries in 1964 was found to be 10.5% of payrolls, with rates ranging from 3% (Burma) to about 40% (Chile). Over and above this main form of tax, one also finds employer contributions to industrial injuries schemes, apprenticeship taxes (e.g. 2% of payrolls in Guinea) and wages taxes (common in ex-French Africa, e.g. 5% in Algeria and 4% in Togo). In some countries these sums represented significant proportions of GNP, e.g. the figure for both Chile and Uruguay seems to have been about 8% in the early 1960s.[1]

There are some obvious advantages in collecting taxes in this way. A payroll tax by definition excludes profits from the tax base and is therefore much more akin to the family of consumption based taxes (retail sales taxes, value added taxes and the like) than to the standard type of income tax. Thus it must be expected to be more conducive to saving than the latter to an extent depending on the interest-elasticity of saving. The correspondence between payroll taxes and value added taxes is not exact (the former is usually levied on an origin and the latter on a destination basis); and we may get a different answer depending on whether an *ex ante* or an *ex post* stance is taken,[2] but it is near enough to regard them as close relations to one another.

As is evident from the figures quoted above, payroll taxes have their appeal to tax collectors as well as to economists. Payrolls of enterprises above a minimum size are not difficult to ascertain and check. Nor do employers always feel strongly about such taxes. This may be partly the feeling that the burden of payment does not fall on them; and partly that in a very roundabout way they may be getting some return for such taxes, for instance, in the form of state pensions for their present or

---

[1] More recent information on payroll tax rates is given by G. E. Lent, 'Tax Incentives for the Promotion of Industrial Employment in Developing Countries', *IMF Staff Papers*, July 1971.

[2] *Cf.* C. S. Shoup, *Public Finance, op. cit.*, Chs. 9 and 16.

future employees in the Social Security case, or in the form of skill-acquisition by employees if the tax is, say, a means of financing training schemes.

Unfortunately, the situation is not quite as idyllic as the discussion so far would suggest. First of all, even if payroll taxes were imposed proportionately on all payrolls without exception, we should have to face the formidable objection that they are likely to encourage capital-using techniques, processes and industries relatively to labour-using ones. This is a difficult and complex subject which we cannot explore fully here[1] but some of the major issues are as follows. Capital costs are often reduced in developing countries by tax measures (e.g. investment subsidies or tariff exemptions) or by credit and interest rate concessions. Similarly, labour costs are often pushed up by minimum wage legislation and similar devices. In a world where one of the most pressing of recent problems in developing countries is *total urban* unemployment[2,3] as distinct from the well-known and long-recognised *partial rural* unemployment, any inducement to substitute capital for labour must be regarded with alarm and apprehension. Nor can one really take refuge in some comforting propositions which are often put forward. One is that a general rise in wage rates will, under certain fairly plausible assumptions (e.g. about interest rates) not affect the relative costs of labour and capital, in that the price of capital goods will tend to increase *pari passu* with that of labour.[4] By and large, this proposition is of limited applicability in developing countries which import substantial amounts of capital equipment: it can be argued that a payroll tax will

[1] *Cf.* A. R. Prest, 'The Role of Labour Taxes and Subsidies in Promoting Employment in Developing Countries', *International Labour Review*, April 1971, and references cited therein.

[2] See D. Seers, 'The Colombia Employment Programme, *International Labour Review*, October 1970.

[3] Recent estimates of *total* unemployment seem to come out at between 10 and 15% of the work force in many countries.

[4] *Cf.* P. A. Samuelson, 'A New Theorem on Non-Substitution', *Collected Scientific Papers* (M.I.T. Press, Cambridge, Mass., 1965), Vol. 1; and E. J. Mishan, *21 Popular Economic Fallacies* (Allen Lane, Penguin Press, London, 1969).

lead to greater imports of such goods, and if this results in devaluation of the exchange rate the price of capital goods will then rise in domestic currency. But this is clearly a much more roundabout and long drawn out process than the simple relationship envisaged above. Another apparently comforting proposition is that there is zero elasticity of substitution between capital and labour on the grounds that in the short run, when capital goods are given, no opportunities for substitution can possibly arise and that in the long run firms will always choose the most modern (i.e. developed country) type of technology. This is a subject which has provoked a great deal of discussion which cannot be adequately covered here. Suffice it to say that there are both theoretical reasons (e.g. that labour taxes may encourage de-casualisation and overtime working) and practical ones for thinking that changes in relative prices of factors will affect the proportions in which they are combined.[1]

So it would seem that there are some serious implications of payroll taxes even if they are of a wholly general character. In practice, of course, a payroll tax will certainly not be uniform throughout an economy. Even if the tax is proportional to payrolls, it is inevitable that small-scale enterprises and self-employed people will not be fully caught; and it would be highly surprising if remote or rural areas were as fully covered as near or urban ones. Reviglio's figures on the proportion of population covered by social security schemes in different countries are sufficient evidence of this.[2] This means that in practice even proportional payroll taxes are highly discriminatory against those firms or industries which are within their ambit. Irrespective of whether these selective payroll taxes result in higher product prices or lower factor rewards – and either result is possible in principle – there will tend to be a contraction of activity and hence of employment[3] in the industries affected.

[1] *Cf.* A. R. Prest, *op. cit.*, p. 330.
[2] *Op. cit.*, p. 510. In 1960 only 2.7% of the population of developing countries was estimated to make social security contributions compared to 23% for advanced countries.
[3] Except in outlandish cases, e.g. if labour were an inferior good, the imposition of a payroll tax could lead to a large enough increase in the use of labour per

In so far as this retards the growth of the modern sector of the economy, this is clearly a matter of grave concern.

Nor is this the end of the catalogue of possible woes. Taxes imposed according to employee numbers rather than payrolls will obviously differentiate more against firms employing large numbers of unskilled men but with the same total payroll as those employing a smaller number of skilled men – a practice hardly calculated to improve the employment situation. An even more bizarre situation arises when social security contributions are used to finance family allowances,[1] a situation which could lead to both a reduction of employment opportunities and the procreation of a larger population in search of such opportunities. There are also international complications in that payroll taxes, unlike value added taxes, are not rebatable under the rules of GATT.[2] Under a system of fixed exchange rates we should therefore expect to see a reduction in the volume of exports (and an increase in the volume of imports) compared to the situation with a consumption tax levied on the destination principle. Finally, it must also be recorded that the collection of payroll taxes may not be as troublefree as one might think at first sight. Both Reviglio[3] and Hart[4] record cases of substantial delays in handing over such taxes to the authorities. And the picture painted by Break and Turvey[5] of the complications of the multifarious social insurance taxes in Greece in the early 1960s should make anyone think before advocating payroll taxes with wild enthusiasm. The scrapping of the 2% general payroll tax in Malaysia at the end of 1970 in the hope of promoting labour intensive activities and reducing unemployment may indeed be a sign of an overdue re-assessment of the merits of this form of taxation in developing countries.

unit of output so that any loss of employment due to a reduction in output is more than offset.

[1] Reviglio, *op. cit.*, p. 513.

[2] *Cf. GATT Basic Instruments and Selected Documents*, 9th Supplement, Geneva, 1961.

[3] *Op. cit.*, p. 519.

[4] *Op. cit.*, p. 878.

[5] G. F. Break and R. Turvey, *Studies in Greek Taxation* (Athens 1964), p. 185 ff.

COMPULSORY LENDING[1]

Compulsory lending schemes, or the compulsory depositing of cash sums with governments on the understanding that such sums will be repaid in the future, can take a number of different forms. One is the type of advance deposit which sometimes has to be paid by importers.[2] The standard characteristics of such schemes are that a deposit, equal to a high percentage of the value of imports, has to be placed with the authorities for a period of a few months, usually without interest. If the value of imports remained constant through time this could amount to an interest-free loan of a given value to the government for so long as the scheme remained in operation; but any tendency for the value of imports to increase through time would add to the size of the loan. As schemes of this kind are usually introduced in times of short period emergency, they can be thought of as being primarily deflationary in character and as being biassed against imports. To the extent that, as a consequence, foreign suppliers grant larger credits to importers to enable them to maintain the previous volume of imports and/or to help with any liquidity difficulties, advance deposit schemes reduce to a method of attracting larger capital imports.

A second type of compulsory lending scheme has a more general coverage than imports, being usually tied to something like the income tax base. There are a number of examples of such schemes in recent years. The usual characteristics are that bonds are issued for periods ranging from five to ten years, interest payments being of the order of 4–5% p.a. (tax free). Normally the sums lent are not deductible for income tax purposes (and correspondingly repayments are not taxable), and the certificates or bonds are non-transferable. Other features sometimes found are lottery prizes instead of interest payments and cost of living adjustments to interest and/or capital repayments. Most schemes have only been in operation for short

---

[1] For fuller discussion, see A. R. Prest, 'Compulsory Lending Schemes', *I M F Staff Papers*, March 1969.

[2] See J. O. W. Olakanpo, 'Monetary Management in Dependent Economies', *Economica*, November 1961, and further references cited there. The UK operated a scheme of this sort from 1968–70.

periods of time. The main reasons for introducing them have been the need for a measure of deflation in an economy and the feeling that, for one reason or another, an element of compulsory lending was preferable to a rise in tax rates or a cut in expenditure. For instance, a rough and ready way of assessing loan contributions (e.g. without any allowance for differing family sizes) may be more readily stomached than similar treatment in the income tax case. Other reasons seem to have been the feeling that by this means some recompense could be made to the heirs of this generation for any burdens imposed now, whereas this is both less easy and less likely with straightforward taxes; the stimulation of capital markets has been claimed as another objective.

A third type of compulsory lending is that associated with employee contributions to national social security or provident funds.[1] The main differences from the earlier categories are that typically these apply to wage-earners, salary-earners, etc, but not to self-employed people, nor to non-wage incomes; that loans are made for much longer periods than in the other two cases; and that pressures on state supported pension funds are often sufficient to ensure a rate of return on employee contributions[2] in excess of what is actuarially justified.

This is by no means a comprehensive catalogue of compulsory lending schemes (e.g. insurance companies may be compelled to hold some of their funds in domestic government securities) but it is sufficient to illustrate the range of possibilities; in fact we shall concentrate on the second of the three cases mentioned in the rest of this discussion, but references to the others will be made where major differences arise. One other observation needs to be made before proceeding further; devices of this sort are frequently called 'compulsory saving schemes'; this is a misnomer for the *lending* which people have to make to governments may or may not be accompanied by additional *saving*.

[1] See Reviglio, *op. cit.*, p. 516, for details of such contributions. We have discussed employer contributions under the general heading of payroll taxes.

[2] Whether the rate of return should be based on employee or total contributions depends on whether one thinks employer contributions are compensated by lower wages than would otherwise prevail.

One of the most recent examples of the second type of compulsory lending scheme is to be found in Ceylon.[1] The scheme was designed to apply to all income in excess of Rs. 6000 p.a. with the exception of employees in the income range Rs. 6000–Rs. 12000 who were being called on at that time to make larger contributions to the Employees' Provident Fund.[2] Government corporations and charities were to be exempted but not companies.[3] The scheme was declared to be a one-year imposition only and interest was to be payable at 5% (taxable). The basis for the assessment was to be total income and the rate of contribution varied from 2% to 20% of income in the case of individuals, rising to 50% on corporate undistributed profits and even higher for 'excessive' dividends. Some concessions were made in respect of wealth tax payments for 1971–2 in view of the additional burden of compulsory lending. The provisions of this scheme were, given the level of existing taxes in Ceylon, more severe than many others[4] but nevertheless they are worth recording as the most recently introduced scheme at the time of writing.

The economic effects of such schemes are complex and can only be analysed by making a number of restrictive assumptions.[5] But if we compare compulsory lending which is proportional to income with an equal yield proportional income tax, it is fairly easy to show that the relative preferences of those subject to the scheme will depend on a comparison of discount rates. First, there is the rate at which funds could have been deployed if they had not been commandeered by the government; secondly, people discount the prospects of future repayment at a certain rate; and thirdly – and this is often forgotten – they will discount the prospects of having to finance the repayment of the loan at a certain rate. Depending on the relative sizes of these

[1] Cf. Budget Speech, minister of finance, 25 October 1970.
[2] The notion that the two are partial alternatives in this case reinforces our arguments for treating both types of compulsory lending under the same general heading.
[3] Companies were exempted later.
[4] Cf. A. R. Prest, loc. cit., Appendix (p. 50), for details of other schemes.
[5] Ibid.

discount rates, the compulsory loan will be nearer to a pure tax or to a pure loan.[1] A rough judgement would seem to be that savings incentives would be much the same under the two alternatives but work and risk disincentives might be somewhat less under a compulsory loan arrangement. There would seem to be no simple summary of the relative equity consequences; these depend, for instance, on the methods of financing repayment of the sums lent.

Once the basis of comparison is broadened so that we hypothesise alternatives other than an income tax, or imagine that the scheme lasts for a number of years instead of being a one-shot operation, we have a very wide range of possible outcomes. But two particular topics of great importance must be discussed. The first is that by comparing a compulsory loan with an income tax imposed on the same group of people, the same total of income etc, we are abstracting from an important possibility: that either type of scheme can deter people from moving out of the subsistence into the monetised sector; or (possibly, depending on the precise tax or loan coverage) from the self-employed to the employed category in the monetised sector. If the supply of labour to paid employment is perfectly inelastic, we can ignore such problems; but otherwise not.[2] So, if, for instance, the comparison is between a compulsory lending scheme applying to a relatively narrow group of people and a system which raises the same amount of revenue by a *per capita* tax imposed on everyone, the picture on work incentives is less

---

[1] Assume that \$1.00 is raised in year 1, and this is repaid in year n with accrued annual interest. The sum involved will be $(1 + r)^n$ where the rate of interest paid (net of any tax liability) is $100r\%$. The present value of such a sum will be $\dfrac{(1 + r')^n}{(1 + r)^n}$, where r' is the subjective discount rate applied to the prospect of repayment. Similarly, the present value of the sum needed to finance repayment will be $\dfrac{(1 + r'')^n}{(1 + r'')^n}$, where r'' is the subjective rate of discount applicable to the finance of repayment. The relative size of r, r', and r'' will determine whether the compulsory loan approximates more nearly to a straight tax or a straight loan; e.g. if $r'' > r'$ (as seems likely) we do not have equivalence to a tax.

[2] *Cf.* Ch. 2 p. 40. This is one of the main problems arising with social security schemes. *Cf.* Ch. 6, p. 119.

favourable than when the comparison is with the income tax.[1] The second issue is that it is frequently argued that in a country with a growing level of money income *per capita* (whether due to rising output or to price inflation) for a given population or with a growing population with given money income *per capita*, or both, the amount of compulsory lending in any one year will tend to exceed the principal repaid, even though rates of contribution remain unchanged. This means that such a scheme would permanently reduce the level of private demand, compared to potential output, below what it would otherwise have been. Similar arguments are often made about social security schemes.[2] This proposition holds if we look at such devices in isolation. But if we revert to the comparison with a proportional income tax and ask what would happen to the yield from that in the context of money income or population increases, it is by no means clear that compulsory lending devices have any net advantage in this respect. Their claims must therefore rest on advantages other than that of revenue buoyancy. No doubt one can find other comparisons where compulsory lending has deflationary advantages; all we are concerned to emphasise here is that one cannot state that this advantage holds as a universal principle.

So much for general analytical issues. How have such schemes fared in practice? The only honest answer is 'not excessively well'. Most of them have been short-lived and yet extensive modifications have had to be made to the legislation during the time they were in operation, e.g. in raising exemption limits or excluding various classes of people from a scheme. Nor can it be argued that they have been an important source of additional revenue in most cases. Ghana raised 10% of her revenue by this means in 1962–3 but this was exceptional; figures of 1 or 2% have been much more common.[3]

---

[1] A *per capita* tax imposed on subsistence producers must of itself be expected to increase willingness to work in the monetised sector.

[2] See e.g. Bent Hansen, 'Tax Policy and Mobilisation of Savings', A. T. Peacock and G. Hauser (eds.), *Government Finance and Economic Development* (OECD, Paris, 1965); F. Reviglio, *op. cit.*

[3] The arguments in this paragraph relate to general schemes of compulsory

At the same time, it is unwise to write off the idea completely, at any rate as a short term device. There does seem to be some evidence that these methods of raising funds are less disadvantageous to incentives than many straight taxes.[1] Provided that certain precautions are taken in the formulation of the schemes (e.g. minimising the link with income tax arrangements, fixing the date of repayment unambiguously instead of leaving it vague, making interest payments annually instead of adding a lump sum at the time of repayment, permitting transferability of bonds) devices on these lines have a useful, if minor, role to play in the finances of developing countries.[2]

BETTING REVENUES

Revenue from betting can either take the form of taxes on commercially run enterprises or that of profits from a government monopoly. Although the latter entails questions of public enterprise which in general are being postponed to Chapter 6, it seems simpler to treat this particular type of government activity here in conjunction with other forms of betting tax.

Although betting taxation can be said to be inefficient from an allocation viewpoint, just like other taxes on individual activities, most people would take the line that any such tendency is offset, and possibly more than offset, by externality considerations. On theoretical grounds it would seem that taxes on 'information betting' (e.g. backing other people's race horses), is likely to yield more revenue than 'zero-information' betting (e.g. lotteries), or 'skill-betting' (e.g. bridge-playing). But on the other hand, a tax on zero information betting is less likely to impair effort than in the other cases.[3] The choice between government enterprise and government taxation of betting is more likely to depend on administrative problems of enforcement and the like than on refined economic principles.

lending and not to employee contributions to social security funds.
[1] *Cf.* A. R. Prest, *op. cit.*, p. 44–5.
[2] For a more pessimistic view, see C. S. Shoup, *Public Finance, op. cit.*, pp. 425–6.
[3] *Ibid.*, pp. 421–3.

We can illustrate the importance of betting as a source of revenue from one or two examples. An investigation into government lotteries[1] showed that there were sixty-six countries in the world where these could be found at one level of government or another. For twenty-three developing countries, the mean ratio of revenue from this source to total revenue was 1.5% (maximum Panama 10.0%).[2] There was a good deal of volatility from one year to another in revenue proceeds; and it was also found that very frequently such revenues were earmarked for social or welfare purposes and not treated as part of general revenue. Both the ratio of prize values and that of operating expenses to total sales varied widely from country to country. Thus net revenue might be anything from a very low figure up to 30% of total sales. Where lottery coupons were tied to retail sales, lotteries had a useful part to play in enforcing the collection of sales taxes – a point also noted by Hart[3] and Shoup.[4]

Another example is the way governments in West Africa have capitalised on African fascination with football pools, e.g. the Western State of Nigeria annually collects a modest but useful sum of revenue from its pool betting tax.

[1] Juanita D. Armstrong, 'The Revenue Importance of Government Lotteries' (1968, unpublished).
[2] Excluding any revenue from taxes imposed on national lottery prizes, as in Honduras.
[3] A. G. Hart, *op. cit.*, p. 837.
[4] C. S. Shoup, *Public Finance, op. cit.*, p. 435.

6
Public Expenditure Issues

The range of topics which have claims for inclusion under this heading is enormous. One could be the determination of the size of the public sector as a whole. This might in turn be discussed in terms of welfare theory, e.g. the theoretical problems of public goods, merit wants and externalities; or one might wish to discuss the role of public sector expenditure in the light of objectives set by a National Plan; alternatively, one might place the main emphasis on any discrepancies between total public spending and that which might be expected, on the basis of econometric analysis, for a country of a given level of income, population, geographical area and the like. A second general area for discussion would be the principles of choice between the main components of public expenditure. This investigation could take a number of different forms: one might argue on traditional utility lines about gains and losses derived from increasing expenditure fractionally in one direction and reducing it in another; or one could employ cost-benefit techniques for judging the relative merits of different expenditure proposals, especially capital expenditures; or one might, in the particular circumstances of developing countries, want to know a good deal about the relative ease of adjusting expenditure levels in the face of any sudden worsening of revenue prospects, due to export adversities and the like. A third area could be the merits of different forms of public intervention: the distinction between public provision (when the government organises production itself or through a closely controlled intermediary) and public supply (where goods and services are supplied at low or zero price to people but are not actually produced in the public sector);[1] and the relative merits of transfers (and their equivalent

[1] There is, in fact, a fourfold division here. Public production can be associated with commercial-type pricing or zero-type pricing; so can private production

113

such as public guarantees of loans) and resource-using expenditures. Another possible subject is the techniques of measuring and controlling government expenditure, including such modern developments as Planned-Programming-Budgeting-Systems (PPBS). Still another would be to analyse the effects of different types of expenditure; this might be primarily to ascertain the input-output relationships in an economy or alternatively to gauge the distinctive income and employment generating effects of specific expenditures via the multiplier process. Interest might also centre mainly on the particular problems arising in the formulation and execution of expenditure under different headings – defence, education, health etc – treating each one *sui generis* rather than looking at inter-relationships with others. Or, finally, one's main concern might be the division of responsibilities between central, state, and local governments.

The need for selectivity in this chapter is obvious enough after detailing this long, but not exhaustive, list of topics. In so far as we shall be dealing with some of them later (expenditure formulation and control etc in Chapter 7; state and local issues, if rather obliquely, in Chapter 8; and small country peculiarities in the Appendix), there is no difficulty. But choice between the others is far more difficult. However, Chapter 1 gives us some leads. We saw there (page 21) that econometric attempts to formulate grand laws of motion in relation to total public expenditure had not been very successful so far. We also saw that in very many developing countries one finds a situation where expenditure is pressing extremely hard against revenue bottlenecks. These two considerations would therefore suggest that it might be wiser to devote our time and space to some individual categories of expenditure and also to ones where some possibilities of charging consumers arise. If one can alleviate the burden of expenditure in this way, this clearly helps in the task

which is bought by the public sector and then distributed to consumers. But one of the four cases, i.e. private production and commercial pricing is less important than the others in that the case for any public intervention in this instance is not self-evident.

of raising revenue by the usual kinds of taxes. In a sense, therefore, the rest of this chapter will be concerned with revenue as well as expenditure matters.

We shall select three areas in the public sector for analysis – social security, education, and public enterprise (with major emphasis on transport). Somewhat different problems crop up in discussing transfer and resource-using expenditures; and similarly with administrative-type and commercial-type expenditures. It is hoped that our selection covers sufficient ground to throw some light on these differences. And in all three cases, there are important questions of charging beneficiaries, in whole or in part, for the services they receive. Finally, we shall mainly concern ourselves with the peculiar and particular problems arising with these types of expenditure in developing countries, rather than with the elements which are common to all types of country.

SOCIAL SECURITY

There are two topics for discussion under this heading: first, the general case for establishing any such system and, second, the particular forms which the contributions and benefits should take. The general case for a national social security system can be based on a number of different arguments. It can be maintained that both very primitive societies and very advanced countries have their own mutual security systems – in the form of conventional obligations on relatives to look after the aged and infirm in the one case and in the form of an elaborate network of taxes and transfers by the state in the latter. If this be so, the argument might run, is it not right to say that there is an *a priori* case for some system, however limited and restricted, applicable to all the intermediate classes of country? Another line of attack is to say that there are fundamental economic reasons why social security expenditure should increase with the growth of income: in so far as such services are purchased in the market there is a high income elasticity of demand for them and so public provision should acknowledge this want accordingly.

Other reasons are also advanced. One is that a national social security scheme can be an important means of adding to the level of public sector saving. This would hold in the building-up stages of a fund even if population and money income per head were constant over time; if either or both of these is rising through time, the argument holds on a permanent basis (see page 110). Another is that social security arrangements may be a means of securing reductions in money wage rates (or at least of lessening the rate of increase) in countries where they are artificially high.[1] And in so far as there is a likelihood of continuing inflation it can be argued that publicly organised pension schemes are more likely to provide some protection against such developments after retirement than the vast majority of private schemes.

Of course, there are arguments to put on the other side. The first is whether one is prepared to countenance an increase in the importance of the public sector relatively to the private sector on this account. Even if total saving were to increase, this might be at the expense of a lower level of private saving. It might also be argued that other government expenditure needs are large enough to strain tax-raising powers without piling on large amounts of transfer expenditures for social purposes. Nor are some of the arguments advanced in favour of social security schemes entirely watertight. Unemployment compensation may be a device for keeping up wage rates rather than bringing them down. And the proposition that the improvident should be compelled to save more than they otherwise would so as to prevent them from being a liability in old age to their more provident fellows implies public compulsion to save – but not necessarily through public institutions.[2] Administratively, it would be impossible in most underdeveloped countries to reach all sections of the population by such schemes. Is it, therefore, fair or even workable to confine them to a few sections?

[1] *Cf.* J. E. Meade, 'Mauritius; a case study in Malthusian Economy', *Economic Journal*, September 1961.
[2] *Cf.* A. R. Prest, 'Some Redistributional Aspects of the National Super-annuation Fund', *Three Banks Review*, June 1970.

Fascinating as these arguments are, this is not the place to develop them further. We can proceed on a` more mundane level by simply acknowledging that, whether one likes it or not, there is a great popular demand and, indeed, world-wide pressure to introduce various types of social security arrangements and that most politicians will not be averse to introducing them.

If this be so the next set of questions is about the form that such schemes should take. First, one can argue about general budgetary provision against an earmarking type of arrangement. This depends partly on one's general view about the merits of earmarking – a subject we shall come to in the next chapter – and partly on the specific point that a system of compulsory lending may be implicit in any such arrangement. If one takes the view that such a system has less disadvantageous effects than outright taxation the case for earmarking is that much stronger.

A second major controversy centres round the case for funding public pension plans. One argument, frequently adduced, is that funding is a 'must' because that is the normal method adopted in private sector pension provision. This is clearly fallacious; the public sector possesses the power to raise taxes or contributions from the present generation of workers to pay pensions to retired people, totally irrespective of whether there is a fund or not. It may be that the existence of a fund is a better assurance of pensions being paid; but even this assumes that such a fund is not raided for other purposes – as has been the fate of many earmarked funds in many countries. Nor does it follow that the size or the time pattern of the excess of revenue over expenditure is any different in one case from what it is in the other.[1]

A third area of controversy is the source of finance of any earmarked system. This is partly a question of taxes on wages versus other taxes; partly the form of any wages tax – whether on employees, or employers, whether proportional to wages bills or to numbers etc. Efficiency aspects (such as work incentives)

---

[1] *Ibid.*, for further discussion and reference to the literature.

are involved here as they are, for that matter, in the details of unemployment, sickness or retirement benefits which are in any way dependent on income from other sources.

A final question is the effects of social security pensions provision on income distribution. This is partly a matter of intra-generation redistribution (e.g. if contributions and out-payments, after allowing for secondary repercussions, confer net benefits on the poorer people in any given generation); it is also a matter of inter-generation redistribution (generation B when active may support generation A when retired; but if generation C is even more generous to generation B when it has in turn retired, we can say that B is a net gainer from the two operations). The detailed results of any given public sector scheme are likely to be very hard to disentangle in either of these respects,[1] though a fair generalisation seems to be that inter-generation redistribution is the more certain outcome of the two.

So much for the general arguments about the role and form of social security schemes. What do we find in practice? Reviglio[2] has investigated this at length and we cannot pretend to add anything to his findings. A large number of developing countries were found to have introduced schemes, whether of a social security or provident fund type. Contributions were very frequently based on payrolls, with employer contributions usually being far higher than those from employees.[3] Benefits took many forms, but their importance in central government expenditure varied enormously from country to country, e.g. 0.4% in Nigeria but 42.0% in Uruguay.[4] The excess of revenue over expenditure (after adjustment for the relevant amount of government contributions) was found to be a substantial component in total saving in some countries, e.g. there were seven out of thirty-one developing countries in which it was over 7% of gross domestic investment.[5] And in some countries the funds were major holders of public debt, e.g. in Uruguay and Malaysia

[1] *Ibid.*, for an attempt in respect of a suggested scheme in the UK.
[2] *Op. cit.*
[3] *Ibid.*, p. 516.
[4] *Ibid.*, p. 508.
[5] *Ibid.*, p. 337.

more than 50% of the total internal public debt was held by them.[1] Finally, one very important conclusion was that an econometric investigation gave some support to the idea that contributions to social security funds and the like were not at the expense of other forms of tax revenue, i.e. such schemes would appear to represent a net addition to taxable capacity.[2]

What conclusions are suggested by this combination of theoretical propositions and practical experience? As far as *benefits* go, one must be even more careful than usual about generalisations as conditions vary so much from one country to another. Nevertheless, one or two points can be made. First, if our arguments about income tax reliefs for children are valid, the case for a national system of family allowances seems pretty weak – unless there are some strict limits to its applicability. Secondly, the difficulties of defining the number seeking work, the number of unemployed or the number absent through sickness make the concept of nation-wide schemes to cope with adversities of these kinds utopian. Inevitably, such schemes can only be partial (e.g. limited to wage earners or to townsfolk) and this immediately implies that the most needy may benefit very little if at all. On balance, it would seem far better to provide floors to living standards by benefits in kind, especially in the form of basic food stuffs and medical supplies. This would reach many of those most in need in the lowest income groups; and it might also help to moderate wage demands in so far as these are influenced by prices of key items in the cost of living. The argument about undue interference with consumer freedom of choice need not weigh too much with us in this context.[3]

The case for public pension provisions is a good deal stronger, given the difficulties of ensuring adequate private arrangements, but all the same there is a lot to be said for restricting such arrangements to the provision of minimum standards; public

---

[1] *Ibid.*, p. 356.

[2] *Ibid.*, p. 536. See also F. Paukert, 'Social Security and Income Redistribution: A Comparative Survey', *International Labour Review*, November 1968, for further factual information about social security schemes in developing countries.

[3] Even so, the population repercussions of such arrangements must be carefully examined.

provision should be thought of as more of a complement to than a substitute for private provision. And whatever else is done, the terms on which older people are allowed to join such a scheme must be carefully regulated; this has been the albatross round the neck of many public sector schemes in many countries.

In discussing the *finance* of expenditures of these kinds, some major considerations have to be remembered. One is Reviglio's finding that the usual social security taxes do not appear to displace other taxes;[1] another is the adverse effects of payroll taxes in promoting capital-intensity etc (see page 103 above). A possible compromise would be to redress the present heavy imbalance between employers' and employees' contributions which one finds in many countries. If, for instance, employers' contributions were cut to something much nearer to employee levels and the balance made up by taxes on value added or even turnover, one might avoid the worst side effects of the present arrangements. It is completely fallacious to assume that an arrangement which is appropriate for countries on the continent of Europe – if indeed, it is fully appropriate even there – should hold for developing countries with chronic labour surpluses and job shortages.

Whether pension provision needs a fully funded arrangement is a nice question. Administrative arguments are clearly against it – and as we have seen, one should attach a good deal of weight to these (see page 116 above). On the other hand, in so far as such techniques are thought to give greater assurance of ultimate payment and as they may have useful side-effects in the development of capital markets and in the pursuit of other policies,[2] the argument probably does go in their favour.

EDUCATION[3]

We saw in Chapter 1 that education absorbed 17.7% of central government expenditure in a sample of twenty-three developing

---

[1] *Op. cit.*, p. 536.

[2] E.g. the government of Malaysia uses its employees provident fund as a control device for grants of tax holidays to new firms employing a minimum number of workers (*cf.* p. 60).

[3] Some of these arguments are more fully developed in A. R. Prest, 'Internal

countries compared to 12.8% in a sample of eighteen developed countries. There is a variety of ways in which one can point up the importance of this type of expenditure. One recent estimate[1] for twenty-three African countries is that public education expenditure takes as much as 30–40% of current government expenditure in some countries in that continent. The average ratio of education expenditure to GNP was put at 4.2% in the mid-sixties, and it must be remembered that this implies a considerably higher fraction of the monetised component of GNP. Moreover, expenditure under this head is growing rapidly: enrolment in primary classes grew at a rate of 4.5% between 1960 and 1965, but this was capped by both the secondary enrolment growth rate per annum (7.5%) and the post-secondary rate (10.6%). In the countries of middle Africa public expenditure on education was growing at a rate three times that of GNP over this period. Nor should it be thought that Africa is entirely unique in these respects as a similar situation can be found in many other countries.[2] Other indications of the importance of this expenditure component are the amount of attention it receives in Development Plans[3] and the number of high level national commissions which have been set up to review the subject in different countries.[4]

It is not difficult to see the reasons for these developments in a qualitative way. It is partly a matter of population growth and especially urban population growth; partly that there is an element of keeping up with the Jones in such matters; but most important of all, a belief in the idea that there are real advantages to be won from the accumulation of human capital: greater physical and mental dexterity, better knowledge of job opportunities, greater willingness to take risks and launch out into

Fiscal Policies and Education Programmes in Underdeveloped Countries', *Financing of Education for Economic Growth* (OECD, Paris, 1966).

[1] See 'Manpower, Education and Training in Africa', *Economic Bulletin for Africa* (UN, Addis Ababa), June 1970.

[2] See *Economic Bulletin for Asia and the Far East* (UN, Bangkok, September 1963), for details on Asian countries.

[3] See e.g. the First, Second and Third Plans for Pakistan.

[4] Pakistan (1959), Nigeria (1960), India (1966), to take three examples only.

new enterprises and new jobs, the hope that more education contributes to the breaking down of antiquated class structures and possibly also the potential effects of slowing down the growth rate of population. Given this list of possible advantages it is not difficult to understand why there are pressures for more public expenditure on education and why politicians yield to such pressures. At the same time emphasis must be placed on the qualitative nature of the explanation. It has not proved easy to disentangle purely economic determinants of education expenditure in developing countries by econometric cross-section methods; it may well be that political and social influences are the over-riding ones.

Whatever the precise reasons for these developments, they are already a major problem for the public finances of some countries, and are likely to become so for others in the very near future; for despite the rapid growth in expenditure in recent years, all indications are that the demands will grow even more quickly in future in many countries. One must therefore try to see what are the most likely ways, whether on the expenditure or revenue side, by which these pressures on government financial resources can be reduced, whilst minimising future reductions in output growth resulting from any current cutbacks.

It would not seem that we shall get very far by looking for some golden rule which will enable us to say how much should be spent in any given country at any given time. There are a number of approaches[1] which can be enlightening: the correlation between education expenditure and income per head; the residual approach which (usually) uses a Cobb-Douglas production function to sort out the contribution of education and research to output growth; the method of estimating returns to human capital expenditure on the basis of expected lifetime earnings; and the manpower needs approach. All these approaches are useful and instructive but they have not yet crystallised into infallible policy guides even in Western-type countries. So it

[1] *Cf.* W. G. Bowen 'University Finance in Britain and the United States; Implications of Financing Arrangements for Educational Issues', *Public Finance* Pt. I, 1963.

would seem that one cannot pin too many hopes on such techniques in developing countries with their incomparably inferior data and the lack of technical expertise to analyse such data as do exist.[1]

Another line of approach is to distinguish sharply between public *provision* of education and public *support* of education. The latter could take the form of issuing vouchers to people to spend on education at whatever primary or secondary school they want, the actual provision of schooling being made by anyone who met certain minimum requirements.[2] Suggestive as such ideas are, they would not seem to be very relevant to the conditions found in most developing countries. They imply a degree of sophistication among users of vouchers which is unlikely to be general; the problems of administration would be enormous – termites have a remarkable appetite for pieces of paper in tropical countries; and, as Bertrand Russell once observed, in discussing J. S. Mill's ideas, the main alternative to state provision might well be church provision, a solution which might be as objectionable to latter day proponents of these ideas as it would have been to Mill. Finally, such proposals would not necessarily reduce the total of government spending, but only its form, that is, from providing goods and services to providing transfers. There may be a good deal to be said for such a change in some circumstances, but it is not much help in the central problem facing us here – how to make a *net* reduction in the total of government expenditure.

In fact there seems to be little alternative to a pragmatic approach. The details must clearly differ from country to country but some broad generalities would seem to hold. As far as relative concentration on different educational stages is concerned, one must look very closely at the provision of

[1] But see M. Blaug, P. R. G. Layard, and M. Woodhall, *The Causes of Graduate Unemployment in India* (Allen Lane, The Penguin Press, London 1969), for a most valuable analysis of Indian educational problems.

[2] *Cf.* A. T. Peacock and J. Wiseman, *Education for Democrats* (Hobart Paper 25, Institute of Economic Affairs, London 1964), for proposals on these lines in the UK context.

elaborate university educational facilities. The phenomenon of unemployed arts graduates is well known; and it is often cheaper to train people abroad (even after allowing for greater 'brain-drain') if very expensive laboratories or equipment are involved; and it is now a by-word that some of Britain's worst legacies to its former colonies were over-elaborate university buildings and over-concentration on curricula which had very little relevance to local conditions. The problems at secondary level are rather different. Although there is clearly a great deal of demand for the kinds of skills which can be acquired there, we do have to face some serious issues of costliness, especially in Africa. Domestic expenditure per secondary school teacher is commonly a much higher multiple of national income per head there than in Western countries.[1] The proportion of total costs represented by teachers' salaries is such that the only possible ways of making economies – or, rather, preventing a costs explosion – lie in reducing the multiple or increasing teacher/pupil ratios.[2] At primary level, the main problem for many countries is how soon they should aim at providing some primary education for all. This is an extremely difficult nut to crack; much as one must applaud the principle of universal primary education, it may be that the provision of teaching facilities and also the necessary enforcement procedure are beyond the scope of many countries for some time to come.

Another issue is adult education. This may be another very hard decision to take. Social and political arguments for devoting resources to such ends are obvious enough; but purely economic advantages are much fewer. One suspects that this is an area where many countries will, however reluctantly, be compelled to hasten slowly. On the other hand, there are two areas which demand expansion rather than contraction. One is

[1] *Total* as opposed to *domestic* outlay per teacher is an even higher multiple but this is because salaries of expatriate teachers are often supplemented from foreign sources.

[2] *Cf.* W. A. Lewis, 'Priorities for Educational Expansion', *Policy Conference on Economic Growth and Investment in Education* (OECD, Paris 1962), and *Development Planning* (Allen and Unwin, London, 1966).

the sub-professional grade of people with *some* knowledge of scientific agriculture,[1] forestry, surveying and the like. The other is the education of women. They often perform agricultural and trading activities in developing countries as well as being the medium by which education can be more readily transmitted to the younger members of a family. So it is all too easy to underestimate the value of diverting more educational resources in this direction.

Other possible moves are to make transfer payments in a number of selected cases; the result may be to reduce the net burdens falling on the public sector. One example is to give marginal financial help to local communities; this may enable them to enlist resources in the form of labour and materials which would otherwise go unused.[2] Grants or tax relief to missions and the like may generate much larger totals of educational expenditure, on the basis of gifts from abroad and local school fees. Similarly, tax reliefs or subsidies to firms which have apprenticeship or training schemes will enlarge the amount of such training; they also tie in with the arguments in Chapter 2 (page 59) about the most appropriate means of assisting firms in countries with high levels of unemployment. Finally, it should go without saying – but unforunately does not – that a great deal can be done in the way of improving systems of government procurement and financial control in this area. The history of the post-war achievements of the educational authorities in the UK in keeping down costs of school buildings by clever architectural planning and building organisation is an example. We shall have more to say on this general subject in Chapter 7.

A number of suggestions can also be made on the revenue side of the accounts. Primary schools charged small fees in England in the nineteenth century; this is also customary in mission run schools in the developing countries today. There is surely some-

[1] *Cf.* K. B. Griffin and B. Glassburner, 'An Evaluation of Pakistan's Third Five Year Plan', *Journal of Development Studies*, July 1966.

[2] Fiji is sometimes quoted as a country which has achieved near-universal primary education, whilst keeping down demands on the central government budget by encouraging local initiative.

thing to be said for the same practice in state or local authority schools, especially when education is often not something which can be provided for all.[1] The same principle holds even more strongly in the case of universities, especially in countries with a surfeit of graduate man- or woman-power.[2]

Services provided for industry or agriculture can also be charged for. Where firms benefit from public provision of technical and vocational training, it seems perfectly reasonable to levy a special charge on them. It would be undesirable to levy such a tax on a payroll basis but alternatives such as turnover, or possibly profits, could be found. And if farmers pay levies for the provision of irrigation or drainage facilities, the same principle can reasonably be applied to public provision of technical agricultural advisory services of various kinds. There are many other possible devices, such as special bond issues or lottery ticket sales, as means of raising funds for school buildings and the like but we shall not discuss these in detail here.[3] We shall, however, have something to say about the general merits of earmarking funds for particular purposes in Chapter 7.

One final topic remains; the division of responsibility between central and local administration. There are some obvious advantages in giving local administrators a good deal of authority in the educational field; they may be able to arouse more interest and enthusiasm among the population as well as attracting more contributions[4] than would otherwise be possible. But such policies are not all plain sailing. Local authorities may take the view that expenditure on mobile human capital is less advantageous to them than expenditure on immobile fixed capital, i.e. one has to think not just of how well education expenditure may fare on a local rather than on a central basis, but also how attractive it is to local authorities relatively to other

[1] *Cf.* U. K. Hicks, *Development from Below* (Oxford University Press, Oxford, 1961), for some account of these matters (e.g. p. 259).

[2] *Cf.* Blaug, Layard, and Woodhall, *op. cit.*, Ch. 10.

[3] *Cf.* A. R. Prest, *loc. cit.*, for further analysis.

[4] E.g. in the form of a surcharge on property, as suggested in Colombia. See R. M. Bird, *op. cit.*, Appendix C.

forms of expenditure. And in so far as widely differing standards begin to emerge at local level, this may necessitate some system of differential grants by the central government, with all the resultant administrative implications.

PUBLIC ENTERPRISE

No discussion on public finances in developing countries would be complete unless it paid attention to this subject. One reason is that public sector commercial type activity often covers a very wide range – not only the traditional Western activities such as transport, communications, water and power supplies, but also some manufacturing and services provision (e.g. banking and insurance). And within any one of these groups government interests may be very extensive, for instance, not only road provision but also public ownership of passenger and freight vehicles. A second reason is that these allegedly commercial activities are often not so, in the sense that in many cases one finds losses rather than profits, thus leading to a drain on government general funds and repercussions at many other points in the public financial system.

The most comprehensive discussion of this latter subject is to be found in the 1968 paper by Gantt and Dutto.[1] Data were analysed for sixty-four public corporations from twenty-six countries, averaged over a seven year period in each case. Tabulations are given of flow of funds ratios (i.e. average difference between current revenue and expenditure – without making any allowance for depreciation – as a percentage of the average of current revenue and expenditure), net income ratios (numerator adjusted for depreciation requirements, denominator as before) and surplus-after-investment ratios (numerator further adjusted for capital requirements for net investment, denominator as before). Confining ourselves for the moment to the mean figure for all countries and all activities, we find ratios of

---

[1] A. H. Gantt II and G. Dutto, 'Financial Performance of Government Owned Corporations in Less Developed Countries', *IMF Staff Papers*, March 1968.

+8.0%, —16.0% and —66.3% in the three cases. In other words, although there was a positive ratio of surplus to turnover if no allowance were made for replacement or additions to capital stock, once allowance is made for these the ratios become strongly negative. To summarise the overall position, every £1 of activity could be said to need external financing to the tune of £0.66; as approximately half this external financing was effected by loans, we can say that every £1 of activity required subsidising from government general revenue to the tune of £0.33.

Naturally, the picture differs a good deal by region and by type of activity. Without going into great detail, it was found that African countries had larger surpluses than Latin American or Asian ones when gauged by the flow of funds measure, but had larger deficits than Latin American (though smaller than Asian) countries on the surplus-after-investment measure. Railways (largely due to Latin America) performed worse than any other activity on the former test; but electricity (largely due to Asia) was much worse on the latter – this no doubt being a reflection of the very different capital needs of the two industries.

Evidence for a single country, Nigeria, corroborates these general findings.[1] Although the electricity corporation and the ports authority (in contrast to the railway corporation) looked fairly healthy on a current revenue and expenditure comparison, the picture did not look nearly as good once allowance had been made for net investment financial requirements. And it must be emphasised that these public corporations were far from negligible when compared with the federal government, whether in terms of revenue intake or capital expenditure.

There is a variety of ways in which attempts to justify such results can be made.[2] First, there is the well known argument that if for one reason or another marginal costs lie below average costs a loss is justifiable on efficiency grounds, i.e. that optimum

[1] Cf. A. R. Prest, 'Public Utilities in Nigeria: Economic and Financial Aspects' Administration (University of Ife, Nigeria, July 1968).

[2] Cf. A. R. Prest, Transport Economics in Developing Countries (Weidenfeld and Nicolson, London, 1969), Ch. 2, for detailed discussion in the context of road and rail transport.

output will only be secured by pricing on the basis of marginal cost. Even if there is no straightforward excess of average over marginal cost, arguments in terms of externalities (affecting either costs or benefits), or in terms of shadow prices can be brought forward in support of running such activities at a loss. If that does not suffice, recourse is then often made to a second-best type of argument, for instance, that although an ideal system might be to charge private car users and public bus users of roads on a marginal cost basis, inability to do the former, whether for political or institutional reasons, would justify running the latter at a loss. If none of these arguments carries conviction, one can also talk vaguely (and the more vaguely, the more plausible it will sound) about the benefits to the growth rate or to the distribution of income, whether by size, or region, or some other dimension.

Even if any one of these arguments were valid in a particular case, there is one overriding question to be faced on each and every occasion; what tax could be reduced or what expenditure increased if the public enterprise were not to run at a loss? And having identified the source of the subsidy as closely as one can (and this may not be easy), further questions must be asked about the efficiency and equity disadvantages of raising money in this way. It may sound very reasonable to supply some publicly produced good or service to moderately poor people at less than average cost; but if even poorer people are bearing the costs of any such transfer the balance of considerations is very different. So even if any of the arguments for loss-making operations were valid, when taken in isolation, there is more to the story than that.

In fact, there obviously are a large number of cases where losses cannot be justified on any of the grounds mentioned – with consequential ill-effects in terms of efficiency (over-usage of existing facilities or over-investment in new ones) or equity (re-distribution away from poor people). To illustrate, any visitor to Ceylon can see that the state of the roads and of publicly run buses leaves something to be desired; but as soon as one realises that passenger road fares remained more or less unchanged for over thirty years after 1939, the explanation of intensive usage is clear. Electricity in Indonesia has been notoriously underpriced for years, with inadequate allowances for capital charges and depreciation etc. Thus in 1969 the costs of supplying each Kwh of electricity seems to have been between 80% and 140% above the price per Kwh. Quite apart from any encouragement to over-consumption and consequent enlargement of investment needs, this particular subsidy could not be remotely justified on equity grounds in that poor people in rural areas did not use electricity anyway.[1] Finally, as an example of official attitudes, the story may be told of an experience in a Caribbean territory a few years ago. It was pointed out to the local treasury officials that the costs of running the government-operated water supply were approximately twelve times the charges to consumers. To this the reply was: 'Water supply is a social service in a hot country'. The retort to that was 'Britain is a cold country but we don't supply fuel free or virtually free – despite all the woolly talk which there has been about nationalised industry pricing'; The official's reply was: 'Yes, but this is a poor country'; and the rejoinder: 'That proves the point' – and there the conversation ceased.

The moral of all this is that a great deal needs to be done in the way of better enumeration and evaluation of costs and better alignment of prices with costs. This means, for instance,[2] that one must cover all current operating costs, appropriate depreciation allowances (a replacement value basis for renewable assets, an alternative use value for non-renewable assets), a contribution towards capital costs of expansion and a contribution towards the costs of public overhead expenditures. It also means that, however much one may want to edge towards a long-run marginal cost basis for pricing,[3] statistical and administrative limitations will mean that in many countries one may

---

[1] Cf. P. McCawley, 'The Price of Electricity', *Bulletin of Indonesian Economic Studies* (Australian National University, November 1970).

[2] See A. R. Prest, *loc. cit.*, pp. 112–4, for more detailed elaboration.

[3] Cf. J. F. Due, *op. cit.*, p. 65n for a cogent discussion of the reasons why a policy of short run marginal cost pricing for roads is unacceptable in developing countries.

well have to be content with an average cost basis for a long time to come. This, of course, does not rule out such devices as peak charges for electricity usage or tolls on tunnels, bridges and the like. Investment principles require appropriate specification of costs and benefits, appropriate discounting, and also a suitable method for comparing rates of return based on surplus criteria, or what profits ought to be worth, with those analysed in revenue terms only.[1]

Some cases will arise where direct charging at a level below average cost will be justified: if, after rigorous scrutiny,[2] such cases are admitted, it is then appropriate to ask whether there are any indirect means of bridging the gap other than by subsidies from general revenue (e.g. with new roads, there may well be a case for taxing consequential movements in adjacent land values).[3] If, in the end, general revenue subsidies are called for, further decisions have to be taken about whether they should be once-for-all, to give an enterprise a breathing space to adjust the scale of its output or whether on a permanent basis; and whether they should fall on the population at large or, say, those in a particular region who derive special benefits from the loss-making operations of the enterprise.

Various accounting and regulatory devices must also be insisted upon. The likelihood of hiding subsidies or losses is less if accounts of what are allegedly commercial enterprises do not form part of the main accounts of government. And some type of public watchdog organisation – whether called a monopolies board or a prices board does not matter – may well be necessary to prevent public enterprises from achieving their targets (whether expressed as rates of return on capital or alignment

[1] If one can lay down a pricing rule, an investment rule, and a target rate of return, it is not necessary to specify all three. Given any two, the third follows. *Cf.* M. H. Peston 'Reflections in Public Authority Investment', A. R. Prest (ed.), *Public Sector Economics* (Manchester University Press, 1968).

[2] E.g. one should not accept the proposition advanced by a senior official in Nigeria in 1968 that any attempt to put up charges on domestic flights by Nigeria Airways would have been a pointless exercise because most of the travellers involved were civil servants. Such an attitude could easily deprive budgeting procedures and activities of most of their meaning.

[3] A. R. Prest, *loc. cit.*, p. 131 ff.

of prices with costs) by exploiting any monopolistic power they may possess to put up prices rather than by reducing costs.

One cannot emphasise too often that public enterprise financing, if not carefully watched or controlled, can easily become the largest canker in the financial system of a country. And once a canker of this sort gets a hold, surgery to excise it requires a combination of dexterity and toughness which is exceedingly hard to find.

7
Legislative and Administrative Aspects

Governments differ from one another in innumerable ways but one universal characteristic is that they prepare budgets periodically (and usually annually). Budgets themselves have a common core, a survey of government finances in the year past and an estimate of them in the year ahead, however much they may differ in other respects. We shall therefore discuss this common core first, as generalisation is likely to be most fruitful here. Subsequently, we shall explore other topics which are important in many countries: the interrelations between the budget and other major economic documents such as a National Plan, the uses and misuses of Planning-Programming-Budgeting Systems (PPBS) and the planning of tax reform.

TRADITIONAL BUDGETING

There are four stages in the budgetary process in any country. First comes that of *formulation* – of making advance estimates of revenue and expenditure – and this is entirely the responsibility of the executive arm of government. Second, we have *authorisation*, the stage at which legislative approval is or is not given to the executive's proposals. Third comes *implementation*, the process of disbursement and collection of funds, this being essentially an executive process. The last stage, that of *postmortem*, is partly an executive and partly a legislative responsibility. We shall now discuss some of the more important issues arising under each of these four headings.

Budget Formulation
The first golden rule of this stage is the necessity for one consolidated statement of estimated revenue and expenditure for the

133

:ntral government. This may seem a very small request but it is
)ne which is frequently ignored. In some cases, even though the
budgetary process does cover everything, expenditure and/or
revenue is estimated (and subsequently legislated) in bits and
pieces, which are not united at any stage. In others, particular
components of expenditure may be left out of the general
budget, being fed from earmarked sources of revenue. A particular example of the latter was the system of subsidising cocoa
production in Trinidad in the early 1950s. At a time when cocoa
had risen to ten times its pre-war price, and other countries
such as Ghana and Nigeria were raising large sums of taxation
from cocoa farmers, a subsidy of several hundred thousand
dollars a year was solemnly being paid to the cocoa industry –
all because a special fund, fed by particular sources of revenue
(import duties, sweepstakes etc), had been set up some twenty
years earlier in totally different circumstances.

Many other illustrations could be given of like phenomena,
e.g. an analysis of the Greek budget revealed over 250 different
funds[1] and in Colombia 37 out of 86 special funds were deriving
their revenues from earmarked sources.[2]

These illustrations bring out the essential reasons why one
has to insist on a single, consolidated and all-inclusive budget.
Without it, one cannot possibly have a unified budgetary policy.
If all revenue does not flow through one single channel, the
temptation to spend in one direction purely because there are
funds 'belonging' to that line of expenditure is only too likely to
triumph over the need to weigh the value of expenditure in one
direction against that in others. In fact, matters may be even
worse, if there is any tendency to relax standards of efficiency
in administration in such circumstances. On these grounds, therefore, one must make a very strong plea for a budgetary system
which enables revenue to be looked at as a whole, and expenditure to be looked at as a whole rather than one which breaks
down each side into a number of pieces or one which matches
specific items of revenue with specific items of expenditure.

[1] *Cf.* G. F. Break and R. Turvey, *Studies in Greek Taxation, op. cit.*, p. 102 ff.
[2] R. M. Bird, *Taxation and Development, op. cit.*, p. 48.

The practice of feeding specially designated funds into a particular channel and of insisting on close correspondence between such revenue and expenditure out of the fund can be defended on a number of different grounds.[1] One[2] is that earmarking may be a better means of registering individual preferences than general fund budgeting. Earmarking can be said to compartmentalise fiscal decisions whereas general fund budgeting is a more analogous to a tie-in sale. The second[3] is that raising revenue by earmarking is likely to be more acceptable to both governor and governed, e.g. a local council can say to its taxpayers that it is, say, levying an extra property rate specifically for the purpose of building a new school. Although justice may be done when taxes disappear into a large central government coffer, it is more likely to be seen to be done and become more palatable, with smaller-scale operations, with taxpayers' names printed on them, so to speak. Another argument, sometimes used, is that earmarking is a way of tying politicians' hands so that they cannot spend revenue in 'useless' ways.

None of these arguments carries overwhelming conviction. The first two are partly antithetical; better registration of individuals' preferences and public sector expansion are not easy to reconcile as policy objectives. The third pre-supposes that there is some means of separating 'useless' expenditures independently of the judgements of those holding political office. For these, and other, reasons one must be extremely cautious about accepting the propositions that specific taxes should be designated for specific purposes and that the amounts of revenue received should closely determine the amounts of expenditure incurred under any one head. There may, perhaps, be some cases at local level when the arguments in favour predominate;[4]

[1] Cf. A. R. Prest, Transport Economics in Developing Countries, op. cit., pp. 145–9.

[2] Cf. J. M. Buchanan, 'The Economics of Earmarked Taxes', Journal of Political Economy, December 1963.

[3] Cf. Sir Arthur Lewis, Development Planning, op. cit., pp. 128–9.

[4] Cf. the proposition that rural populations demand public services but are more willing to pay taxes or contributions for such services if local, rather than

but at central level they are likely to be few and far between.[1]

There is one general exception to this principle. Where the government is responsible for commercial operations, it is highly important to account for them separately. This will increase the likelihood of more rigorous application of commercial accounting principles and will also bring out into the open any elements of profit or loss. In so far as various administrative departments of government perform miscellaneous functions similar to commercial operations and collect fees therefrom, it would seem reasonable to allow revenue of this kind to be kept by the departments with a corresponding reduction in their appropriations rather than go to the trouble of routing it through the finance department.

Given the necessity for a single comprehensive budgetary statement, what form should it take? The most important single point in underdeveloped countries is whether capital expenditure should be rigidly separated from current expenditure, but there are others as well, e.g. should expenditure be classified on a functional basis or on the basis of the spending department responsible, should revenue be classified according to whether it is deemed to be at the expense of private saving, or private consumption, and so on? Perhaps the ground can be cleared a little if we first look at some classifications which are not very sensible. The first is the distinction we often find in ex-British territories between ordinary expenditure and development expenditure, the latter being prepared by a department responsible for a development programme or something of the sort. This does not seem to make much sense and results in an

central, authorities are involved. See comments by Sir Arthur Lewis in H. M. Southworth and B. F. Johnston (eds), *Agricultural Development and Economic Growth* (Cornell University Press, Ithaca, 1967), pp. 493–6.

[1] *Cf.* M. C. Taylor, 'Taxation and Economic Development: a Case Study of Peru', *Inter American Economic Affairs*, Vol. 21, No. 3, p. 47. 'This earmarking of such a high proportion of revenue prevents an orderly and intelligent budget procedure, reduces the authority and responsibility of Congress and frustrates the implementation of development programs. Earmarking of revenues also constitutes a built-in guarantee that government expenditure will rise regardless of the need for the services.'

essentially arbitrary separation of expenditures – with the implicit (and most probably wrong) connotation that nothing in the ordinary budget has anything to do with development and that everything in the development budget has something to do with it.[1] Another false distinction is to differentiate between different sorts of capital expenditure according to the source of finance, e.g. to put such expenditures in different watertight compartments depending on whether it is financed by grant, by loan or from revenue surpluses. Practices of this kind often stem from the idea that by analogy with business enterprise, loan receipts have to be used for capital expenditures as otherwise the necessary interest to service the debt will not be forthcoming. This, of course, is fallacious; the guarantee of paying interest on loans resides in a government's power to raise taxation and not to the future returns on the particular expenditure made from the loans. It may be that a condition of raising a loan, especially from abroad, is a demonstration that national revenue is likely to rise sufficiently to ensure that the payment of interest and amortisation will not present undue difficulties; but this again does not necessitate meaningless accounting procedures. Similarly, the proposition that capital budgets should be arranged to show changes in the net worth of a government is devoid of analytical content.[2]

It would seem that the case for capital budgeting – and for that matter any particular classification of revenue and expenditure – must really rest on whether it helps the government in its functions of policy-making and management. The commercial distinction between capital expenditure (with attendant depreciation provisions) and current expenditure is of dubious relevance in a large area of the public sector[3] – no one has ever satisfactorily explained why the costs of school building but not

[1] *Cf*. P. T. Bauer, *Indian Economic Policy and Development* (Allen and Unwin, London, 1961), p. 129. 'The identification of development with development planning is a fundamental and pervasive flaw of much current discussion on this subject.'

[2] *Cf*. R. A. Musgrave, *The Theory of Public Finance, op. cit.*, p. 562.

[3] It must be remembered that we are excluding public commercial enterprises from the main government accounts.

those of teachers' salaries should be regarded as capital formation; or what is the appropriate basis for depreciation provision
on the Houses of Parliament at Westminster! It could be vitally
necessary to know the total of government capital expenditure
in any particular year but that is a different matter from saying
that it must be accounted for completely separately from current
expenditure. If it can be accounted for separately without
obscuring the distinction between physical capital formation
and loan transactions, all well and good; but if the result of a
capital budget is to blur this distinction it is not clear that there
is any net gain from such a presentation.

Essentially the same principles apply in taking other decisions
about the classification of revenue and expenditure. If, for
instance, government policy-making requires detailed information about inter-industrial relationships in an economy, its own
expenditure data will have to show the breakdown between
spending on major commodity groups. Similarly, the question
whether government accounts should be drawn up on strict
national accounting lines, distinguishing between public receipts
and payments according to whether they correspond to income
or capital transactions of the private sector, depends on the
system of parliamentary control. If, for instance, it is important
for the legislature to know the outcome of a financial year
immediately after the end of that year, a cash accounting system
(as distinct from the usual commercial accounting basis) is
inevitable. Essentially, therefore, answers to these questions
must depend on the particular circumstances of a particular
country.[1]

The next consideration is the time horizon for budgeting.
There are several sub-questions: the length of any one budgetary
period (twelve months, or more, or less), the number of such
periods considered in any one budget and the methods of linking
one set of estimates with another. We shall have more to say on
these subjects later (see page 150) and so let us concentrate here

[1] In so far as the donors of international aid insist on separate accounting in
respect of their gifts, the receiving country does not have the last word and it may
be forced into a classification which is not optimal from a budgetary standpoint.

on the first question – the length of any one period. It is some-times argued that one can avoid all problems of expenditures straddling different periods by extending lengths of periods. This is clearly not so: however long the period one takes, one can still have projects being started at the end of it and over-lapping into the next one. One must also remember that differ-ent projects need very different lengths of time for their execution and so the accounting period appropriate for one type of ex-penditure is simply not suitable for another. On the whole it seems best to stick to the traditional twelve month cycle, to examine long term commitments extremely carefully at the initial stage (see page 150) but then to regard the annual account-ing procedures as much more of a formality in subsequent years. But one is only too well aware that this is more easily said than done.

The final point under this general heading of budget formula-tion is to stress the importance of close estimation. Some investi-gations over a twenty-four year period (1930–53) in the Carib-bean area showed that there were large errors of estimation, with a strong tendency to underestimate both revenue and expenditure and the former relatively more so than the latter.[1] A more recent exercise for Colombia also showed substantial errors; in the direction of over-estimation on the revenue side and underestimation on the expenditure side.[2] The large dis-crepancies between these sorts of findings and those for a country like the UK[3] can be explained either in terms of deliberate policy, or the difficulties of accurate forecasting in the light of frequent unexpected changes, or incompetence. Whichever be the correct mixture of explanations in any given case, the general principle that no government can hope to execute its economic policies successfully if its budgetary forecasting is wildly in-accurate seems clear enough.

[1] A. R. Prest, *A Fiscal Survey of the British Caribbean* (HMSO, London, 1957), pp. 114–15.
[2] R. M. Bird, *Taxation and Development*, op. cit., pp. 46–7.
[3] A. R. Prest, 'Errors in Budgeting in the UK', *British Tax Review* (Jan.–Feb., 1961); see also C. M. Allan, 'Fiscal Marksmanship, 1951–63', *Oxford Economic Papers*, July 1965.

Budget Authorisation

The authorisation process does not call for lengthy comment. If the budget is prepared as one single consolidated statement, discussion by the legislature is likely to be far more to the point than if it is not. The main difficulty is to ensure that adequate parliamentary discussion takes place and that the result is neither a rubber stamping nor a complete reversal of the executive's proposals. It would be idle to pretend that advanced countries have solved these questions satisfactorily: in the UK there has in recent years been an increased tendency to rubber stamping and in the US there is always the opposite problem of mutilation of the executive's proposals. Some sort of happy mean, perhaps with widespread discussion in the legislature in general terms, whilst committees do the more detailed work of examining estimates, is no doubt the ideal solution. But, inevitably, the actual application of it must differ from country to country. Finally, it goes without saying that, as far as revenue legislation is concerned, slipshod formulation of regulations or unquestioning copying of foreign legislation is often worse than useless.

Budget Implementation

There is rather more to discuss under this heading, especially on the revenue side. We shall take that first and come to expenditure later.

We have already alluded to the likelihood of tax evasion in a number of cases, e.g. the loss of income taxation in rural areas or among small traders, and the loss of import duties due to undervaluation or smuggling. We are now more concerned with the general principles of improving tax assessment and collection than with the detailed applications in particular cases. Professor Shoup[1] has set out the relevant principles in some detail. To mention a few: the amount of tax due is not always fixed with complete certainty and there may be a zone over which a taxpayer can quite legitimately argue for ('protest' in Shoup's terminology) a lower figure than the tax collector demands; nor is it self-evident that tax authorities should always try to

[1] C. S. Shoup, *Public Finance, op. cit.*, Ch. 17.

maximise the revenue they collect as distinct from, for instance, ensuring that no one group of taxpayers has a higher rate of evasion than others. When it comes to the principles on which action should be taken, there is a certain element of choice between tough enforcement of the rules to secure tax payment and heavy penalties if, in fact, the appropriate amount of tax is not paid at the appropriate time. It seems fair to say that no country would rely on one of these two strategies and neglect the other entirely; in practice, one would expect to see something of both – though when one looks at the systems prevailing in some countries, expecially in Latin America (e.g. very low interest rates on late tax payments; a positive eagerness not to prosecute offenders) one might be pardoned for thinking that they do not follow either strategy.

Two further general points must be made. The first is that in countries where unemployment, complete or partial, is rife the opportunity cost of arguing about tax dues is low. Systems of tax enforcement which give wide opportunities for objecting to assessment by hard-pressed tax collectors must therefore be regarded with some misgivings. Secondly, a number of writers[1] have recently drawn attention to the particular problems of tax collection in conditions of persistent inflation. Taking first the case where money incomes stay constant through time, the taxpayer's gain from deferment which does not attract any penalty is equivalent to a permanent loan at a rate of interest equal to the (net) rate at which he could have borrowed from the market. If there is a penalty on tax deferment, the annual gain is equal to the difference between the net market rate and the penalty rate. If money incomes rise through time, the sum 'borrowed' rises through time and presumably at a faster rate than incomes if there is a progressive tax structure. In so far as the market rate of interest tends to rise in money terms as inflation proceeds but the penalty for late payment of taxes

---

[1] See R. M. Bird, *Taxation and Development*, *op. cit.*, Ch. 3; A. G. Hart, 'Fiscal Policy in Latin America', *op. cit.*, p. 864; and T. Hirao and C. A. Aguirre, 'Maintaining the level of Income Tax Collections under Inflationary Conditions', *IMF Staff Papers*, July 1970.

remains unchanged (or is not immediately adjusted) the annual rate of return in money terms will also rise through time – so that the taxpayer gains both through increases in the principal and through increases in the relevant rate of interest.[1] With rampant inflation this state of affairs can be serious both in terms of costs to the revenue authorities[2] and in terms of inequity between taxpayers with differing possibilities of deferment. Needless to say, it is easier to analyse than to cure the malady. But there would seem to be two obvious moves to be taken: the first is to get as much tax payment as possible on to a current year basis and the second is to ensure that penalties for late payment are kept in line with interest rate changes and applied where due – without further delays.

When we come to the detailed ways in which tax assessment and collection can be improved, there are a number of standard devices. One is a greater exchange of information between all the relevant departments.[3] Another is to put some weight on more self-assessment; but it should be remembered that examination of this proposal in the context of land taxation (see page 92) did not suggest that it won very high marks. We may note that in Lord Hailey's *African Survey*[4] there is some mention of the technique of paying tax collectors a percentage of their takings. For instance, the income tax (i.e. near poll tax) operating in Bechuanaland up to 1938 was collected on this basis. Significantly enough it seems to have had a more successful history than a similar sort of tax – but *not* collected on a commission basis in Swaziland.[5] This seems to be a possible way of operating a rudimentary tax system and far more likely to achieve reasonable results than more complicated devices. One would have thought that many of the countries we are covering could have explored it with profit, at any rate in the initial stages of levying personal taxes on a widespread basis.

[1] Alternatively one can express these arguments in terms of real and nominal tax rates. *Cf.* Bird, *op. cit.*, p. 248.

[2] Delays in payments to government creditors could be an offsetting item.

[3] *Cf.* Ceylon Budget Speech 1970–1, Colombo, Oct. 1970.

[4] *Op. cit.*, third edition, 1957, pp. 654–5.

[5] *Ibid.*

Another device is that of retailers issuing coupons to consumers, stating the value of the tax paid. The coupons are
subsequently redeemable, at something less than face value.
This may be a way of administering a retail sales tax tolerably
efficiently and yet relatively cheaply. However, this pre-supposes
that a retail sales tax is a practicable possibility and this is by
no means universally so. Yet another system is that of using
informers and rewarding them well.[1] But there are clearly very
strict limits to any such system.[2]

There is one other suggestion in this field which deserves
some attention. In his *Indian Tax Reform*[3] Professor Kaldor put
forward proposals for a revenue system which was designed to
be self-checking (in the sense that if the taxpayer falsified information under one head, he would have to pay more tax under
another). These proposals have been taken up and elaborated
further by Professor Higgins.[4] In the latter version, it is proposed
that a tax system should consist of a personal income tax, a
company income tax, a general sales or turnover tax, a (variable)
tax on all assets including cash, a tax on excess inventories and
a personal expenditure tax: given a system of this sort, it is
claimed that virtually all loopholes are closed and no taxpayer
can get away with underpayment of tax.

As a set of logical propositions, a system of this sort no doubt
has its attractions. One can also agree on the urgency of reducing
tax avoidance and tax evasion to reasonable proportions and
on the desirability of reducing backlogs in tax collection. But
there seem to be at least three objections of fundamental importance. First, there are the administrative implications. To make
the system work it is suggested that, in addition to complicated
returns by individual taxpayers, one can adopt such devices as
sample physical checks on goods passing in and out of the ring

---

[1] *Cf.* Ceylon Budget Speech 1970–1, *op. cit.*

[2] *Cf.* C. S. Shoup, *op. cit.*, p. 435, 'An informer system must be used in
moderation if a society is not to generate intolerable animosities among its
members'.

[3] *Op. cit.*, Ch. 6.

[4] B. Higgins, *Economic Development* (Norton, New York, 1959), Ch. 23; see
also A. G. Hart, *op. cit.*

within which these taxes apply,[1] sales slips for retail transactions, a system of reporting all sales of assets (including, presumably, motor vehicles), some reliance on public informers[2] and a computer to do the donkey work. The amount of effort needed to make such devices work is so appalling that it is impossible to know where to begin in criticism. But it does seem permissible to point out there are such mundane problems as records disappearing through human negligence (and it is surprising how negligent people can be with unfavourable evidence!) and retailers who are illiterate and so on. More generally, if there were any hope whatever of making such a system work, would not these devices be commonly found in advanced countries already? How can it possibly work in underdeveloped countries where honest and efficient administration is probably the scarcest of all resources? However, it is always easy to laugh proposals to scorn on the vague charges of administrative complications; and so one should not rest all one's case on them. The second charge against such a system is on incentive grounds; it is significant that although Professor Higgins is at some pains to argue that his system would contain incentives to invest (the tax on capital equipment would be at a lower rate than that on liquid assets)[3] there is nowhere any mention of incentives to work rather than to stay idle or remain in the subsistence sector and so further out of reach of the tax system. There is no need to go again into the relationship between taxes and incentives to work. But one needs a great deal of convincing that an all-embracing system devoid of safety valves would not be strongly disincentive in communities just emerging into modern economic life.[4] And on

---

[1] In fairness, it should be made clear that it is not suggested that the system could apply to the whole of the population.

[2] 'To assist in the detection of such cases [unreported sales] informers should be offered a portion of the tax take', Higgins, *op. cit.*, p. 529.

[3] It is not clear, however, how personal saving is to be encouraged. On the one hand, there is an expenditure tax, on the other a set of taxes on capital assets. It is not certain that the net outcome would be an increase in the level of personal saving.

[4] The following judgement has been made on India: 'The simultaneous imposition of several direct taxes – the wealth tax, the expenditure tax, the gifts tax and the capital gains tax – instead of helping check evasion, seems actually to have

a more general plane one would hardly expect such a system to work without a good deal of arbitrariness and uncertainty; is such a background conducive to the confidence necessary for undertaking long-term investment? The third, and in the last resort most important objection of all is the political one; that a system which needs the amount of information prescribed could not fail to degenerate into an inquisition. In fact, one might as well say that the authorities should simply put pistols to people's heads with the words, 'You pay £x in tax or else . . .' It would not really be much nearer to a police state than the above system – and a great deal less expensive to administer.

We can conclude, therefore, that a system of this kind is a nice logical toy but administratively impossible, economically ill-conceived and (for most people) politically unacceptable.

As far as the implementation of the expenditure side of a budget is concerned, the main requirements are that there should be strict control in the spending departments (so that spending really is in conformity with what has been sanctioned by the legislature) and that the treasury should be able to crack the whip over the other departments as necessary. These results are achieved in the UK by the system of making the civil service head of a department responsible for the accounting in his department, by strict treasury control over the conformity of actual spending with what has been voted, and by the activities (e.g. continuous auditing within departments) of the Comptroller and Auditor General – a direct appointee of the Crown and in no way subservient to the government of the day. There are other means of providing the necessary checks, but they must inevitably follow the same general principles. This is certainly a point at which the clear supremacy of the treasury over other departments is absolutely vital.

Budget Post-Mortem
This is the point at which the arrangements in many countries

acted as a psychological spur to greater evasion' (R. J. Chelliah, *Fiscal Policy in Underdeveloped Countries*, second edition, Allen and Unwin, London, 1969, p. 173).

are most deficient. The first pre-requisite is the rapid completion of accounts at the end of an accounting year. Obviously, as with any large organisation, this must take some months, but it is sometimes of the order of years[1] rather than months before such data are available. The next stage is the compilation of the auditor's report, where again considerable delays may occur. Finally – and this is where the worst deficiencies are to be found – there should be adequate parliamentary examination of past expenditure. In the UK we have found over the years that there is inestimable value in having a committee on public accounts which has the power to examine spending in great detail and cross-question the officers of the spending departments as mercilessly as any prosecuting counsel. No doubt there are other alternatives, but without both a detailed examination of some accounts by a committee and a general discussion of all of them by the legislature as a whole, the system of financial control is incomplete. And in both these respects the legislature in many countries does not perform its duties as it should.[2]

The system of financial control may seem to some an esoteric and to others a dry-as-dust subject. But in countries where there is a strong tendency to place on governments responsibilities which are either entirely new or have in the past been in the hands of private enterprise, it is more important than ever. The best will in the world on the part of the executive to control public expenditure is no substitute for a system which really checks to see that it does. There is also another point. Public interest and understanding of the finances of government is often lacking in these countries: without it, one cannot hope that a country's finances will be run as well as they should. But one way of developing and encouraging public interest is for the

---

[1] E.g. the Accountant-General's foreword to the Malaysian data for 1965 was dated 31 December 1967.

[2] *Cf.* International Bank, *The Economic Development of Libya* (Johns Hopkins, Baltimore, 1960), p. 93, 'At present the Federal Parliament and the Legislative Council exercise only the most perfunctory control over the spending of public money'.

legislature to show that it takes an interest itself by full debate and discussion, at all stages, of the financial process.[1]

WIDER BUDGETARY HORIZONS

There is plenty of scope for argument about the ways in which governments should extend surveillance of their finances beyond the traditional type of budgeting. One way of approaching these wide issues is to start by endorsing the general principle that governments should plan ahead in the sense of looking into the future as well as at purely current events. There is no reason why exception should be taken to this; business firms have forward plans for capital expenditure and other commitments stretching into the future as well as budgets for the current year, and governments should clearly not do less. It is quite stupid to pretend that one can conduct the affairs of any long-continuing large economic organisation in any other way.

The next point is that it should be the duty of a government today to concern itself not only with the financing of its own operations but also with the wider development of the economy. This implies the preparation of national accounts showing the level of output, income and expenditure and their division into the various components – consumption, investment and so on. Nor is it just a matter of preparing these accounts in relation to years which have passed. If a government is to guard against short-term inflationary or deflationary tendencies, or take measures to help the longer term growth of the economy, it must prepare estimates of these relationships for future years. One way of thinking about such forward estimates is to regard them as a general framework against which government policies have to be judged. If, for instance, future projections show that the supplies of goods and services are likely to rise by 4% p.a. but offtakes are likely to rise by $4\frac{1}{2}\%$ p.a., this will be a warning

---

[1] For a recent review of US practices see *Report of President's Commission on Budget Concepts* (US Government Printing Office, Washington D.C., October 1967). See also U. K. Hicks, *Development Finance* (Clarendon Press, Oxford, 1965), Chs. 7 and 8, for further discussion of the whole subject.

that some restraint must be exercised if inflationary developments are to be avoided. Estimates of this sort may also be extremely valuable in showing the longer term effects of government spending. Without forward estimating, it is all too easy to authorise government expenditure in Year 1 which is perfectly reasonable in the context of that year, but which will have implications for Year 2 that are far less acceptable. For instance, a health or education programme based on any given size of population may look very different in the context of a population larger in size or different in age or sex composition; and it is not usually too difficult to make short-term predictions of such changes. Nor is it simply that the government's own operations are more likely to be rationally conducted if one looks ahead – the public availability of the best possible estimates of future trends must be of enormous help to businessmen, too, in planning their operations. Forward estimating of both the government's own financial position and of the main items in the national accounts can be justified many times over by arguments such as these. But it is most important to keep one's sense of proportion in the process. First of all, even those countries with advanced systems of economic and statistical intelligence have not had a glorious record in predicting future developments. One of the best known examples here is the famous forecast of post-war unemployment which was made in the USA towards the end of the Second World War; but this experience has been repeated many times over – so much so that it is unnecessary to refer to other supporting evidence. If this is the experience of advanced countries, are there any reasons for thinking that the underdeveloped are likely to be more successful? As far as statistical intelligence is concerned, the count against them is likely to be heavy – there can be no doubt about that. It might, however, be argued that countries of this sort have much simpler economies and that it is much easier, in principle, to predict the future in their case. But this argument is not acceptable. As no one would be foolhardy enough to claim that foreign trade is easily predictable (and still less so, if a country relies heavily on one or two exports), presumably it rests on the assumptions that the remainder of the economy is of a simple subsistence pattern and that it does not change over the years. If these are the assumptions, one must say that they are very frequently inadmissible; the network of internal domestic trade in, for instance, African territories can be extremely complex and in many countries there is a rapid rate of change of income even though the absolute level is still low.

We must not give the impression that government forecasters have a monopoly of inaccuracy of estimation – there is no evidence that businessmen do any better! But the simple point is that the world is a wildly uncertain place and so one should not be deluded into taking forecasts of the future too seriously. If one thinks of such efforts as supplying a broad canvas against which the more reliable current data have to be considered, one is more likely to be realistic than if one considers them as an infallible guide to large-scale action. There is no doubt an underlying psychological appeal in 'comprehensive planning for the future' especially to the less advanced elements of society. This is all the more reason for being properly sceptical of such ideas.

It must be noted that our argument so far – the preparation of forecasts of government and national income and expenditure for periods of more than one year ahead, but with some insistence on not taking such data too seriously – carries no implications one way or the other about the degree to which, or the methods by which, government should intervene in the economy. The setting of national targets, the form and extent of government intervention (e.g. controlling private capital and current expenditure as a whole versus discriminating between different components), the techniques it should use (e.g. fiscal and monetary measures versus physical controls versus public enterprise) are largely political[1] decisions; and they are quite distinct in principle from the decision to undertake forward estimation. It may well be that in practice the borderline between 'forecasts' and 'plans'

---

[1] The proposition that bold planning has purely economic advantages in arousing mass enthusiasm and/or leading to full employment of resources has been severely criticised by P. T. Bauer, *Indian Economic Policy and Development* (Allen and Unwin, London, 1961), pp. 99–102.

is often blurred and indistinct and even that the undertaking of the former may be an easy stepping-stone to the latter. But in principle there is a real difference and so it does not seem altogether illogical to call a halt at this point and confine our discussion to a narrower area.

Within these confines, there are two matters which particularly need discussion: the preparation of estimates of public revenue and expenditure over and above those for the year ahead and contingency arrangements for stabilisation purposes.

Forward Estimates
As the UK is at present in the forefront in this area it may be useful to say something about the system which has evolved there in recent years, without, of course, suggesting that it is applicable without modification to any other country.

The starting point of these recent developments is usually taken to be the Plowden Committee Report of 1961[1] which emphasised the need for regular surveys of public expenditure as a whole (i.e. all central and local government expenditure and capital formation by public enterprises) for a period of years ahead. These ideas were gradually developed during the 1960s and since 1969 a regular procedure has evolved.[2] No doubt this will be changed in the future but the fact that the system survived a change in government in 1970 is some evidence of its attractions to administrations with very differing attitudes to economic policy.

The system is that the government publishes a White Paper about the end of each calendar year setting out public sector expenditure for the preceding financial year (i.e. April–March), the current financial year and the four ensuing ones, with more detail being provided for the earlier than for the later years in the survey. The coverage and the classification of expenditure are

[1] *Control of Public Expenditure*, Cmnd. 1432, HMSO, 1961.
[2] See *Public Expenditure: a New Presentation* (Cmnd. 4017, HMSO, 1969); *Public Expenditure 1968–9 to 1973–4* (Cmnd. 4234, HMSO, 1969); *Public Expenditure 1969–70 to 1974–5* (Cmnd. 4578, HMSO, 1971); *Command Papers on Public Expenditure* (Third Report, Expenditure Committee 1970–1, H. of C. 549, HMSO, July 1971).

quite specifically arranged to be identical with single year data published in other documents. In addition, there is a breakdown between expenditures using up real resources, those which are merely transfers and those which involve changes on capital account. The whole series is cast in terms of constant prices; every year there is a rolling adjustment of the period covered and the price basis is similarly shifted forward by one notch. One or two further points are worth mentioning. A contingency allowance is expressly included in the estimates; and a very real innovation is to be found in the concept of the 'relative price effect'. This is an additional element of notional expenditure designed to allow for the fact that because of differential productivity changes the prices of goods and services consumed by the public sector tend to increase through time relatively to others. In other words, even if public expenditure and GNP were both to increase at the same rate in terms of conventional constant price series, there would be an increase in the ratio of public expenditure to GNP, when both are expressed in current prices.

There has been less consistency in the projection of revenues but when a similar exercise has been performed on that side of the account it has taken the form of a constant price estimate of revenue yields in future years on the assumption that tax rates, allowances, etc remained unchanged. This enables one to compare the likely developments of expenditure with the prospective tax yield on the basis outlined.

How does this new system link with the traditional budgeting system? The situation is complicated in that the form of the latter in the UK has also changed in important ways in recent years but a fair summary would be as follows. The annual budget estimate of expenditure for the year is related to the public expenditure forward look, but not so closely that there is no flexibility to deal with unexpected developments. And in the last resort it is the budget which is the legal authorisation for disbursements of funds. The distinction between a document which is meant to be a survey or guideline and one which is a means of authorising expenditure is emphasised by making them the subject of entirely different parliamentary debates, at different times in the session.

A number of features of this approach to forward estimates are worth noting. First, it does try to shed some light on the trends of government expenditure and revenue and thereby give both government officials and external commentators a better sense of perspective. It should be particularly noted that expenditure is specified separately for each year; it is not just a matter of saying that a sum of £x is to be spent on housing, education or whatever it is at unspecified times over the next few years. Secondly, there is a good deal of latitude about the precise form of the documentation in which such figures could appear: it may be a document dealing solely with the public sector, as in the UK, or it could be part of a wider survey of developments in the economy at large. In either case, it is perfectly possible to build links at both legislative and executive levels between this document and the annual budget so that the latter can fulfil the role of implementing the former. At the same time, one should not think of the UK system as one to beat all possible systems: quite apart from the doubt about the treatment of revenue projections, there are some awkward issues of providing bridges between the different price levels used in successive expenditure surveys and between those in the expenditure survey and budgetary calculations. Finally, as emphasised earlier (see page 139) one is bound to have problems of some expenditures straddling successive expenditure surveys, even when they cover several years at a time.

Stabilisation Measures
We have emphasised the susceptibility to short term cycles and consequential revenue fluctuations in many developing countries, usually due to balance of payments changes (see page 26).

It is easy enough to say that such a situation cries aloud for built-in stabilisers, fine tuning with tax rates and transfer payments and a shelf of investment projects (screened in advance by cost-benefit techniques) ready for immediate adoption if need be. But blanket policy prescriptions of this sort ignore some extremely awkward facts. First, evidence has now accumulated that the records of Western countries in employing such techniques have been far from impeccable.[1] This is largely a matter of mistiming changes in tax rates, etc – 'too little and too late' or 'too much and too soon' – but there is also some recognition that some measures may make for a great deal of waste and inefficiency, e.g. stop-go building operations on public projects.[2] If this is the general experience of Western countries, it seems most unlikely that developing countries, with very limited resources in terms of statistical and economic expertise, could hope to do better. Secondly, even if one were prepared to trust to luck about the capacity to operate in this way, one still has to ask whether such policies are very relevant, when the usual source of a downswing is a decline in the value of exports, whether due to a change in demand or a crop failure or some cognate reason. In this sort of situation a government deficit cannot be financed by internal borrowing without running risks of generating inflationary pressures or balance of payments disequilibria or both. Such results are not inevitable (e.g. if government borrowing mops up funds which would otherwise have gone abroad) but they are sufficiently likely to make one hesitate a great deal before endorsing such policies.

All in all, other lines of domestic policy would seem to be more appropriate in many cases. The most obvious is for a government to accumulate surpluses in 'good' years – both in the sense of budgetary surpluses and foreign exchange surpluses. As income from exports falls in a 'bad' year, the government by drawing on its balances, can kill two birds with one stone – maintaining its own expenditures irrespective of any reduction in tax revenue and without recourse to net internal borrowing; and at the same time releasing the foreign exchange to prevent large falls in the level of imports. Needless to say, there are plenty of difficulties in such proposals. They will almost certainly require deliberate action; and there is always likely to be a built-in bias towards treating an upward deviation from the

---

[1] *Cf.* B. Hansen, *Fiscal Policy in Seven Countries 1955-65* (OECD, Paris, 1969).
[2] Plowden Committee *Report, op. cit.*

trend of revenue receipts as if it were on the trend line and increasing expenditure accordingly. Consequently, one cannot assume that even an income elastic tax system will automatically throw up revenue surpluses in 'good' years.

Another idea[1] is to try to construct a country's tax system so that the income elasticity of tax yield is greater for an upward than a downward movement of money income. Thus the export tax on rubber in Malaysia is set on a sliding scale related to price if this is above a certain level but not if below it – with the consequence that the tax yield depends on both volume and price if the latter is above the critical level, but otherwise on volume only. Devices of this sort surely have a great deal to commend them. One needs a high elasticity of tax yield with respect to money income for both upward cyclical and long term reasons; but many governments would be helped, rather than hindered, if this degree of flexibility did not apply in downward cyclical situations.[2]

PLANNING-PROGRAMMING-BUDGETING SYSTEMS

Before discussing the part which PPBS can play in government finances in developing countries, one must try to encapsulate its essentials. This is not an easy task as some of its more enthusiastic exponents have claimed so much for it that it is difficult to know where to begin, let alone end. The core features seem to be as follows:

1. An emphasis on the output rather than the input side of government spending; this involves a series of programmes designed to achieve various major objectives.
2. An emphasis on a multi-year approach.
3. Cost-effectiveness analysis to discover the most economical methods of fulfilling given functions; and cost-benefit comparisons between alternative proposals.
4. Systematic post-hoc checking of performance.

[1] *Cf.* C. T. Edwards, *Public Finances in Malaya and Singapore, op. cit.*, p. 374.
[2] For a discussion of the role of external assistance in such circumstances see G. Lovasy, 'Survey and Appraisal of Proposed Schemes of Compensatory Financing', *IMF Staff Papers*, July 1965.

The weights attached to these different ingredients differ from one country to another. To date, the USA has been more interested in the analysis aspects; the UK in the multi-year approach; and Canada in the reclassification of budgetary expenditure involved in the first component. No doubt these differing developments reflect weaknesses, imagined or real, in previous systems of budgetary management and control as well as the interests of those charged with the application of these concepts.

How far developing countries should be encouraged to climb on this fast-rolling bandwagon is a matter about which there can reasonably be disagreement. But several things are fairly clear. One is that PPBS is by no means a cut and dried matter, as the sketchy survey above shows. In particular, there is room for controversy about output classification (e.g. should education expenditure be classified on a primary-secondary basis or a science-arts basis?); and as for performance checking, this is more easily talked about than done. It is one thing to compare cash sums estimated with those actually spent; it is an entirely different order of problem to compare output achievement with objectives. So it is fair to ask advocates of these techniques exactly what they have in mind in any particular application. Secondly, the benefits of PPBS will depend on the existing systems of budget accounting and control. It is significant that the most spectacular success was scored in the Pentagon in the early 1960s; significant for two reasons, one being that there were considerable deficiencies in control before the new system was introduced and the other that there is some evidence that PPBS has a more clear cut application in the military field than in others. So the case for application to any given country must depend on its present system of control and on what are the major constituents of budgetary expenditure. This immediately brings us back to our earlier proposals for forward looks and other improvements on existing budgetary processes, such as cost-benefit analysis of major projects. If these can be put into effect and if there is a reasoned linkage between the forward looks and the annual budgetary allocation, it may well be that many of the advantages claimed for PPBS will already be within a country's grasp. Just as Molière's M. Jourdain spoke prose without knowing it, so would countries be incorporating many features of PPBS without involving the name. Finally, all changes of these sorts have their costs as well as their benefits. In countries where statistical talents are scarce the former may be extremely high, especially in the initial change-over stage, e.g. from resource to output budgeting. The fact that Western countries have on the whole proceeded rather cautiously in this, developing one side at a time rather than operating on a broad front, is surely sufficient evidence that developing countries should not lose their heads and rush ahead thinking that this is a modern kind of philosopher's stone.[1]

TAX REFORM PLANNING

This subject is of very great importance but nevertheless the main points can be made quite briefly. It would seem that one should not expect too much in the way of immediate tax reform from missions or commissions which recommend large-scale reconstruction of tax structures. Quite apart from the obvious fact that the appointment of any such commission may be a delaying tactic to ensure inaction for as long as possible, the shortages of experienced and trained tax administrators set severe limits to the immediate implementation of far-reaching reforms.[2] No doubt there are exceptions where particularly persuasive experts have cajoled administrations into extensive legislation; but some of the gilt disappears from this gingerbread when one takes account of the lackadaisical way in which such reforms are often put into practice and of the legislation which, despite its alleged initial promise, has to be repealed for one reason or another within a year or two. Venezuelan experience illustrates another common situation. Professor

[1] For further discussion see R. O. Khalid, 'Fiscal Policy, Development Planning and Annual Budgeting,' *IMF Staff Papers*, March 1969.
[2] One shudders to think of the consequences in the Latin American country which is alleged to have dealt with this by calling in a large number of university teachers.

Shoup and his colleagues presented a carefully worked out report in 1959[1] but it was possible for an observer to report in 1968 that although there had been extensive legislation in the intervening years, there was very little correlation between this and the recommendations of the 1959 mission.[2]

Rather than a once for all re-codification of the tax law, it would seem that tax reform must be on a piecemeal basis, proceeding at a pace governed by the capacity of the administration – and the taxpayers – to absorb it. This does not mean that wide-ranging reports are inappropriate but simply that the rhythm of implementation must be fairly slow. At the same time the need for rhythm must be emphasised – without a continuing programme, the whole process could lose purpose and shape. These general principles lead in turn to some fairly obvious administrative demands. A permanent tax research unit is one; perhaps even more important is the need for governments to announce their tax reform plans well in advance so that people know what is envisaged and major tax changes can receive adequate (though not too much – this is an opposite danger as recent Canadian experience shows) discussion before they reach the statute book. This would seem to be an extremely simple and obvious maxim; but there are so many cases where it has been neglected that one must not miss any opportunity of repeating it.

CONCLUSION

There is one last general question to consider. What ought the role of a finance department to be *vis-à-vis* the other departments of government? Ought it to be analogous to the role of the UK treasury, which, in peace time, plays a preponderant role throughout the process of departmental estimating and spending and in the formulation of government economic policy as a whole? Or should the administrative pattern for underdeveloped

---

[1] C. S. Shoup, *et al.*, *The Fiscal System of Venezuela, op. cit.*

[2] E. F. Gittes, 'Income Tax Reform: the Venezuelan Experience', 5 *Harv. J. Leg.* 125 (1968).

countries be closer to that found in the UK in both the First and Second World Wars, when supremacy lay with the departments primarily responsible for the war effort?[1] If the former were the case we should expect to find the finance department more powerful than the planning department (or development department, or whatever it is called) and *vice versa* in the latter event. Correspondingly, the relative importance of financial control and procedure is likely to be greater in the former case than in the latter.

The answer must surely turn on the extent of government intervention in the economy and the techniques used for this purpose. If a government confines itself to holding the ring and removing obstacles to development of and by the private sector, the traditional supremacy of a finance department is not in doubt. If, on the other hand, a highly bureaucratic and planned economy is the order of the day, the role of the planning department is going to be far more important. But if the latter is the case, it must be remembered that the analogy with wartime administrative organisation is far from close: in wartime one has a very limited range of production objectives, one can impose controls over the individual which are far less easy to put across in peacetime in a democratic country, the effort is for a relatively short period of time and considerations such as balance of payments difficulties do not arise when there is an organisation like Lend-Lease. Development, on the other hand, is usually a long, slow, uphill pull and in such circumstances it is, for instance, much less easy to impose tight controls on consumption, labour etc; and there is a limit to the extent to which the balance of payments can be rescued by emergency measures – as various countries have found out in recent years. Therefore, even in a highly planned economy, the role of the finance department cannot be forgotten for long, at least when there is any semblance of democratic government. The final point to

[1] It may be recollected that in 1915 Lloyd George gave up the post of Chancellor of Exchequer to become Minister of Munitions – an organisation which initially consisted of two men, a table and a desk – but which ultimately became the key department on the war front. And in the Second World War the Chancellor of the Exchequer was not always a member of the War Cabinet.

make is that from an administrative view the worst situation of all is when there are two 'empires', neither supreme over the other and each having its own plans for expenditure. This is sometimes the case in underdeveloped territories where we find a minister of finance budgeting for ordinary revenue and expenditure and a development minister with his separate programme and financial proposals for development expenditure. The fundamental objection to such a situation is that from a fiscal viewpoint the economy is indivisible and so it is quite impossible to drive with two horses in harness at the same time. This notion of indivisibility was a lesson which Britain has had to learn on two occasions since the Second World War. It is much better for countries not to learn this lesson by the hard way of repeating mistakes of this sort.

8
Regional Financial Issues

INTRODUCTION

As the Appendix is concerned with the particular financial issues of small countries, we shall be mainly concerned with larger ones in this chapter. We shall select two aspects of regional finance for discussion: first, the need for special fiscal measures to cope with regional disparities in income levels, growth rates etc, and secondly, the principal problems of central-regional financial relationships under a federal constitution. The interest in the first question in Western Europe and North America in recent years[1] is evidence that there is a subject for discussion, potentially even if not currently, in many developing countries; and even though the post-war movement to federation has suffered some reverses (e.g. the British West Indies and central Africa) the fact remains that India, Pakistan, Nigeria and Malaysia, among developing Commonwealth countries, still retain this form of constitution. It should be noted that there is some overlap between the two topics. For although some federal-state relations require discussion even in the absence of untoward regional[2] differentials and, similarly, the latter require discussion under unitary constitutions as well as a federal one, there will nevertheless be cases where the tinder for federal-state conflagrations is to be found in regional disparities. We shall try to allow for this overlap as we go along.

One or two other lines of demarcation need mention. The first is that we shall not be primarily concerned with the relative development of rural and urban areas. Analytically, the two

[1] See for example, A. J. Brown, 'Surveys of Applied Economics: Regional Economics with special reference to the UK', *Economic Journal*, December 1969; and G. McCrone, *Regional Policy in Britain* (Allen and Unwin, London, 1969).

[2] We shall think of regions in this chapter as being synonymous with the states in a federation.

questions are distinct: financial aid to a stagnant area might be directed to urban or rural pursuits; similarly help to rural activities might benefit either prospering or stagnant areas. Policies may, of course, coincide but they need not do so. By the same token, we shall not be primarily concerned with the distribution of any given size of urban population between small and large cities, though once again there may be positive correlation between policy requirements in this area and those in the more purely regional one. It will be obvious from this that we shall not concern ourselves specifically with local authority matters, as distinct from those of states or provinces.[1] Finally, we may from time to time have to discuss various aspects of revenue and/or expenditure which have not received detailed attention in the preceding chapters.

REGIONAL INEQUALITIES

The central question is whether any special fiscal measures are likely to be needed in developing countries to mitigate regional inequalities in levels or growth rates of income per head. It may be helpful to lead up to this central question by a brief review of the problem in more advanced countries.

The Pattern in Western Countries

It is common to find a whole series of special regional measures in Western countries. These are sometimes in the form of direct controls (e.g. embargoes on location of new factories in some areas), sometimes mainly of a monetary character (loans at subsidised rates of interest) and sometimes fiscal (special investment incentives or labour subsidies of various kinds). Thus the UK, for instance, had had policies of this kind applying to the outer parts of the country for many years; the experience of successive Italian governments in trying to help the southern part of that country are also well known. So are those of Canada in trying to promote activity and growth in the Maritimes.

[1] See U. K. Hicks, *Development from Below* (Oxford, 1961), and *Development Finance* (Oxford, 1965), for extended discussion of local authority matters.

If we ask why this need for special measures arises, the answer seems to be in three parts. First, there are demonstrable inequalities of income per head, employment, work force participation and so on between different regions. These disparities may always have existed, as in southern Italy, or they may be due to the relative decline of once prosperous areas; e.g. the northeastern part of England traditionally relied heavily on a few industries such as coal-mining and shipbuilding, but new industries have not been attracted on a sufficient scale to absorb the labour released as the old ones declined. Secondly, the combination of 'normal' public sector activities and competitive forces has been insufficient to cure these ills. It is important to stress the word 'combination': one can always argue that one of these two components could have done the trick on its own but was thwarted by inequality-promoting forces generated by the other component. Thus one might argue that general government measures would have sufficed but that the process of 'cumulative causation' in the private sector offset, or more than offset, the first set of influences; or that a laissez-faire type of arrangement could also have produced a solution, but that government actions militated against this. Without immersing ourselves in this sea of controversy, it is worth noting one or two common fallacies. If a government has a system of helping declining industries, this is not the same thing as a specifically regional measure: one can have declining industries in prosperous regions; and other regions may be backward precisely because they have never had any economic activity which could suffer a major decline. Nor is it the case that extensive public welfare or anti-poverty programmes will suffice.[1] Even though such expenditures may eliminate gross inequalities of personal income between regions they do not necessarily solve unemployment problems in all areas if large parts of any additional spending are on goods and services supplied from other regions. Lastly, the concept of government measures must in this context include not only those which involve purposive decisions,

---

[1] For a somewhat different view see R. A. Musgrave, *Fiscal Systems, op. cit.,* p. 312.

but also those which are automatic or semi-automatic. By this we mean that there is a regional built-in tax (and expenditure) system as well as a cyclical one.[1] If the income of one region declines many of the tax payments to the central government will automatically fall and the expenditure of the central government in that region will tend to rise (e.g. through more unemployment compensation). These changes will therefore be a partial offset to the decline in regional income. So when one talks about 'normal' private and public measures being insufficient to cure regional imbalances, it is essential to keep this element of the apparatus in mind as well as discretionary ones.

The third reason for needing regionally oriented policies is the feeling that regional inequalities cannot be left as they stand. This may be argued on economic grounds e.g. the loss of output due to higher unemployment in the more backward regions or the fact that a higher level of output can be achieved with a lower rate of inflation if employment is more evenly spread between regions.[2] Alternatively, there may be extremely strong local political pressures at work. It should be noted that the latter often rule out the resolution of inequalities by migration from poorer to richer areas. Regional political feelings are unlikely to be assuaged by programmes which would cure local diseases by transferring all the patients to other geographical areas. There are other reasons why migration may be unacceptable as a main solution but this would seem to be the one which is the most decisive of all. It still remains true in some cases (e.g. the more remote isles of Scotland) that the way to deal with spatial inequalities is to encourage complete evacuation. What we are saying is that there is a severe political limit to the number of cases in which the solution is applicable.

So our lightning glance at the Western scene leads to the conclusion that special regional policies are adopted by many

---

[1] *Cf.* N. Kaldor, 'The Case for Regional Policies', *Scottish Journal of Political Economy*, November 1970.

[2] I.e. non-linearity of Phillips curves will mean that the extent of the rise in wage rates will be less in the (stagnant) regions in which unemployment is reduced than the fall in wage rates in the (prospering) regions in which unemployment is increased.

governments to combat regional inequalities which 'normal' processes do not eliminate and yet which cannot be allowed to persist.

The Developing Country Case

We now have to inquire whether the kind of picture etched above is relevant for developing countries. It is easy enough to show that regional inequalities do exist in many developing countries as well as in Europe or North America;[1] though perhaps it would be more accurate to say that the extremes of regional inequality, as measured by income per head, are greatest in the semi-developed type of country such as Brazil and Colombia, rather than in those at the bottom of the ladder.[2] But the demonstration that inequalities do exist is only the beginning of the story; the next question is whether such inequalities are due to the same sorts of causes as one finds in more advanced countries.

There are certainly some points of similarity. It is just as possible for inequalities to arise in low income as in high income countries, through the working out of natural resources or through shifts in the pattern of demand. In addition to permanent changes of this sort, there may well be short term or cyclical fluctuations which have differential effects on regions. And the probability of having remote areas which are potentially viable but at the moment lack population or capital in one form or another is likely to be greater than in many economies of a more highly organised character, e.g. the Guayana region of Venezuela[3] or North-East Brazil.

There are also some cases which are strikingly different from the archetypical regional problems of Western countries. One is that inhospitable areas, which are best not cultivated, may be more widespread in tropical than in temperate climates. Policies

[1] See for instance, J. Williamson, 'Regional Inequality and the Process of Economic Development', *Economic Development and Cultural Change*, Vol. XIII, No. 1, Pt. II, October 1964.

[2] *Ibid.*

[3] *Cf.* J. Friedmann, *Regional Development Policy: a case study of Venezuela* (M.I.T. Press, Cambridge, Mass., 1966).

to combat the inequalities between such regions and the other parts of a country would be completely misguided. Second, and very important, is the well known emphasis on concentrating new developments in particular areas in order to reap various advantages of external economies and the like – the principle of polarisation, as it is sometimes called. In so far as development policy is very frequently diverted towards creating inequalities of this kind, there is clearly no case at all for a regional policy to combat *all* types of inequality, irrespective of their causes. We are not here concerned with the details of any concentration on the development of some selected regions and still less with the justification for such policies. Our point is simply that spatial inequalities arising for this reason are likely to be much more common in developing countries than in Western ones and so the application of regional correctives needs to be on a highly selective basis.

Having established that not all regional inequalities in developing countries are undesirable and that some may be highly desirable, we must now inquire whether 'normal' market forces and government policies are likely to be sufficient for the undesirable cases. Here we enter into a welter of controversy about how well competitive forces work and about the regional implications of various government policies. It is impossible to generalise here with any degree of safety but the following pointers should be noted. The ease of labour migration can be hotly debated: on the one hand, there are clearly many cases in which people have moved from unpromising, derelict or moribund areas; on the other hand, differences of race, tribe, language etc, can easily set severe limitations on labour movement. As far as government policies go, it is highly likely that built-in regional fiscal mechanisms will be less effective: partly because the ratio of taxes collected to income tends to be less and partly because highly progressive income taxes (the main ingredient of high marginal rates of tax systems of Western countries) are often a relatively unimportant component in the tax-mix. Also, other government policies which bear tangentially on regional inequalities (e.g. anti-poverty policies) are less in evidence than in Western countries. To repeat, these are no more than straws in the wind about a vast subject; but for what they are worth, they would seem to suggest that 'normal' forces are unlikely to be markedly effective catalysts in this context.

Echoing our discussion of Western countries, the next question is whether residual regional inequalities matter. Here there does seem to be one overriding consideration. We saw that regional political discontent was likely to be taken seriously in Western countries. The whole subject is clearly much more explosive in large developing countries where groups of people with very different origins, background and tongues may have been only recently joined together in political wedlock. Dangers of divorce through incompatibility of temperament always exist; when economic cruelty is also present, the strain may be altogether too great. Writing in 1971, one obviously thinks of Bangla Desh, the former East Pakistan, as a prime example. So even though the sophisticated economic arguments commonly found in Western Europe (non-linearity of Phillips curves, for example) may not be a very pressing reason for taking residual regional inequalities very seriously, the issues of political cohesion are likely to be overwhelming and overriding.

So we have now to ask which types of regional economic policies are likely to be most apposite. It is perhaps easiest to start by listing inappropriate policies. On the basis of our previous arguments (see Chapter 2, page 59 and Chapter 5, page 103), one must be careful not to endorse policies which increase the overall differentiation in favour of capital goods or against labour. This means that one must examine rather carefully the way in which special treatment might be given in respect of capital subsidies or labour taxes. A reduction in payroll taxes in disadvantaged regions would be more acceptable than an increase in more prosperous ones, for instance. Another snare is the proposition that one can help disadvantaged regions by devoting more resources to education and training; the obvious danger is that better education improves mobility and there is then an efflux of qualified people to the more prosperous regions

– in the same way as many Welsh teachers and Scottish docto.
have traditionally migrated to England.

It is much easier to say what should not be done than to lay down hard and fast rules about what should be done. One suspects, however, that in programmes of this sort the improvement of communications – roads, railways, ports etc – will almost always have a part to play. No doubt there are many other devices, but their relative importance must vary from country to country. Thus, for instance, Brazil has experimented with tax relief for profits re-invested in the North-East or Amazon regions;[1] and there is a good deal to learn from Mexican experience.[2] Examples of this sort could be multiplied. All that one can really say with any certainty is that there is a wide variety of possible measures and the choice between them must very much depend on the degree of sophistication of the fiscal, monetary and public expenditure systems – in just the same way as it does when the main objective is deliberate promotion of desirable regional inequalities rather than the reduction of undesirable ones.

To summarise, we have argued that there are likely to be some instances of regional inequalities needing special government measures in developing countries. Some types of inequality should be a matter for approbation rather than censure; and some may conceivably be mitigated through the 'normal' workings of the economy. But others are likely to fester if left alone. One final addendum needs to be made; even if the less developed countries are not yet thought to have problems akin to those of the more derelict areas of Western Europe, it is surely important for them to realise that these can occur, to watch for their occurrence and to take appropriate combinations of preventive and curative measures.

[1] Cf. A. O. Hirschman, 'Industrial Development in the Brazilian North-East and the Tax Credit Scheme of Article 34/18', Journal of Development Studies, October 1968.
[2] Cf. D. Barkin and T. King, Regional Economic Development (Cambridge University Press, Cambridge, 1970). For a discussion of some doubtful cases of regional differentiation see L. Lefeber, 'Regional Allocation of Resources in India', P. N. Rosenstein-Rodan (ed.), Pricing and Fiscal Studies (Allen and Unwin, London, 1964).

FEDERAL FINANCES

We may start by outlining the basic political features of federation and its main economic characteristics. We can then move on to the financial inter-relations between the federal and the unit governments, dealing with both the problems which arise when a federation is launched and those which are likely to develop in the course of time. We shall be mainly concerned with current account transactions, but will also cast a glance at debt and monetary matters.[1]

Political and Economic Features of Federation

The classical definition of the political nature of federalism as formulated by Professor Wheare is that there should be a division of powers between the federal and the unit governments, each of which, in its own sphere, is co-ordinate with the others; each government must act directly on the people; each must be limited to its own sphere of action; and each must, within that sphere, be independent of the others. Although the first two of these points are still generally acceptable it has been argued[2] that the latter two are no longer fully applicable to some of the older federations and are certainly inapplicable to some of the newer ones. Whereas in the nineteenth century, the constituent governments were essentially independent of one another, both financially and otherwise, this is no longer true. Today it is much more common to find unit governments partially dependent financially on the central government and the latter frequently shaping its financial policy in order to promote developments in matters which are, constitutionally, the prerogative of the regions. It would, therefore, seem appropriate not to define federalism quite so tightly as formerly and so to admit of a greater degree of administrative co-operation and smaller

---

[1] For authoritiative discussion of these matters in recent years see U. K. Hicks *et al.*, *Federalism and Economic Growth* (Allen and Unwin, London, 1961); and A. Adedeji, *Nigerian Federal Finance: its Development, Problems and Prospects* (Hutchinson, London, 1969).

[2] A. H. Birch, *Federalism, Finance and Social Legislation* (Oxford, 1955), especially pp. 305–6.

degree of independence between the federal and the unit governments.

One reason why the forms taken by federalism in the new states differ from the classical ones is that whereas the USA, Canada and Australia were all countries in which the federal government grew out of the unit governments ('federalism by aggregation'), we have had the reverse situation in post-war years. In India, Pakistan and Nigeria we have federations which have grown out of former unitary colonial-type structures ('federalism by devolution'). Although there are various other forces working in the direction of more co-operation and less independence between constituent governments, the importance of this particular one should not be underestimated.

To explore the economic characteristics of a federal area it is necessary to begin with a fundamental distinction. In principle, we can compare the economy of any given geographical area, which is at present federally governed, with what it would be if the same area were split into a number of independent states. In the case of Nigeria, for instance, we can take the alternative to be either a unitary government covering the whole country or twelve entirely separate governments running the various states. Unless one is clear about these two possible bases of comparison, it seems impossible to make any pronouncement whatever in this field. At the same time it must be recognised that this is a conceptual and not a historical distinction. We are more concerned to ask what the alternative would be to a federation, which is already in existence, than how it arose. In the case of Nigeria, the more relevant comparison for these purposes may be the alternative of a number of states despite the fact that the present federation has arisen from devolution rather than aggregation.

Suppose we consider first the alternative of a single unitary government covering the whole country. In such a case it is very difficult to see any ways in which a federal constitution *must* imply different economic characteristics, other than that there will be an additional layer of government. This is very likely to imply a greater usage of real resources in administration, but even here the precise effect must be entirely dependent on the particular constitutional arrangements of any country. It is possible to imagine circumstances in which there would be vastly greater bureaucracy, but one can think of others in which change would be almost nil. Another possible result is that the multiplicity of governments may render national economic planning less effective than if there were one single government able to enforce its will on the whole country. Whether this is, in principle, an advantage or disadvantage is a subject that must be left on one side. The historical evidence on what happens in practice is somewhat conflicting. It was argued that the existence of four governments in the former Central African Federation hindered development planning but, on the other hand, there does not seem to be much evidence that the Indian Planning Commission has been thwarted in its efforts by the federal nature of the Indian Constitution.[1] The most general verdict seems to be one of 'unproven'.

If the alternative to federation is a series of small states, the comparison is more complicated. Some false arguments must first be refuted. It is sometimes alleged that if a number of states are joined together in a federation, there will be economic advantages stemming from the free flow of goods between them, the unrestricted migration of labour, the economies of a common monetary system (e.g. pooling foreign exchange) and so on. But it is quite clear that these are not advantages of federation *per se*. There are plenty of cases of customs unions or unrestricted migration of labour etc, without federation (there is an easy flow of labour from the Irish Republic to the UK, but one cannot think of two countries less likely to federate); and there are cases (e.g. the former British West Indies Federation) of federation without the benefits of customs unions or free flow of labour. We need not spend any more time on these arguments as their general invalidity is obvious enough.[2]

[1] See, for instance, D. T. Lakdawala, 'The Four Finance Commissions of India', *Indian Economic Journal*, January–March 1966.
[2] It may, of course, be true in *specific* cases that a customs union etc, is also unobtainable if political conditions do not permit federation.

As far as the public sector is concerned, we have, as before, the contrast between a system with three layers of government – federal, state and local – and one with only two. Whether the former must involve a larger real cost of administration is a moot point, however. Although there is no very clear evidence about economies of scale in government administration,[1] it would seem sensible to think that there must be some occasions on which they can be important. A particular case which springs to mind is Nigeria where one has a number of states each endeavouring to administer an income tax system of its own. It would seem reasonable to suppose that one unified system for the whole federal area would secure economies of administration.[2] When one takes points of this sort into account, it seems very doubtful whether one can make the generalisation that the administrative costs of running federal countries will be greater than those prevailing in a series of small countries. It is perfectly conceivable that the opposite could be the case.

As far as national economic planning is concerned, there is one way in which a federally administered area will be at an advantage compared to 'Balkanisation' (or should it be 'Africanisation' these days?). The larger the area the less likely is it that adversity (e.g. low export prices) in one part will be accompanied by adversity in another. How important this will be in practice will depend crucially on the size of the constituent areas, their economic diversity (both inside each area and relatively to other areas) and so on. But it is clear that this is a point of substance. Another comparison is between the borrowing facilities open to a federally administered area and those available to a series of small governments. Even though there is a free flow of capital both inside the area and with the rest of the world, it would seem highly likely that a federal government would be able to borrow more cheaply than unit governments. One of the tasks facing any federation is to see that the most is made of any such advantage.

[1] *Cf.* E. A. G. Robinson, *Economic Consequences of the Size of Nations* (Macmillan, London, 1960, for International Economic Association), pp. 223–40; see also the Appendix.

[2] *Ibid.*

This survey of the economic characteristics of federally administered countries will have made it clear that the *inherent* differences from countries with unitary governments are very small. The main financial issues can, therefore, be discussed in the knowledge that the economic differences between federal and unitary states spring mainly from the existence of an additional layer of government.

Federal Finances

It will be convenient to start a review of the principles and practices of federal finances by hypothesising that a federation is about to be established, whether by devolution or by aggregation, and that a solution has to be found to the financial relations between the constituent governments. Although, in principle, we might equally well expect to find that there was an excess of revenue over expenditure at the state level and a shortage at the federal level or *vice versa*, it is, in fact, the latter situation which has been the common one historically, i.e. an excess of expenditure requirements over revenue intake at the state level. The reason for this is simply that revenue from import duties is normally allocated to the federal government, this in turn being the logical outcome of having a customs union and a common external tariff which is federally administered.[1] As import duties tend to be a larger fraction of total tax yield in relatively underdeveloped countries, it will, therefore, follow that the federal government will have a large slice of total tax revenue. Unless the nature of the federation is such that an even larger share of total spending falls to the federal government, this must imply an excess of revenue over expenditure at that level and *vice versa* at the state level. Although it is conceivable that in the case of federation by devolution there may be a very strong central government, this possibility seems much less likely in the case when the federation is formed from a number

---

[1] It may be noted that although it was originally proposed that the federal government in the West Indies should collect all import duties, this was not the final solution adopted. It seems reasonable to think that this decision was bound up with the continuance of individual tariff structures by the units.

of previously independent states. We must, therefore, expect to find a substantial initial imbalance in such cases.

In due course further financial problems are likely to arise. First, there may be changes in the relative positions of the federal and the state governments. There are several points to distinguish here. First, there will be some forces tending to make federal revenue grow more quickly than state revenue. This might follow, for instance, from the concentration of company taxation in the hands of the federal government as it is highly likely that the corporate sector will grow relatively faster than the non-corporate. Secondly, it may well be that state expenditure will grow more rapidly than federal. For either or both of these reasons we may very well find as time goes by that we have an increase in the federal surplus, or the states' deficits, or both. And even if federal and state revenue and expenditure all increased at the same rate through time, we should find a growing imbalance if the starting position is one of federal surplus and state deficits.[1] In older federations the main trouble has been the disproportionate growth of expenditure on social services. In so far as this has been a state responsibility this has led to a general strain on state finances; and in so far as there has been a trend to nationwide uniformity of social security benefits this has meant greater than average financial strain for the poorer states in a federation.

This brings us to the implications of differing rates of growth among the various states. First, the various constituent elements of a federation are likely to develop at a different rate, some growing faster than others. Even though the free flow of goods and factors from one area to another in a federation may help to prevent very large regional differences in the rate of growth of income per head, some differences will still persist and these will have at least two financial consequences. First, there will in all probability be government revenue and expenditure gaps of

[1] See C. T. Edwards, *Public Finances in Malaya and Singapore, op. cit.* Chs. 11 and 12 for an account of these problems in Malaysia; and R. J. Chelliah, *Fiscal Policy in Underdeveloped Countries* (second edition, Allen and Unwin, London, 1969), p. 208, for discussion on India.

a different order to those which prevailed initially, the areas with the faster growth in incomes benefiting (both for revenue and expenditure reasons) relatively to the others.[1] Secondly, those units which develop least rapidly are highly likely to demand assistance of one sort or another from the federal government – and possibly even from their more prosperous neighbours. Any initial financial settlement is scarcely likely to remain appropriate in circumstances of this sort.

There are a number of possible ways of coping with any initial or subsequent imbalance between state revenue and expenditure. The first is to provide from the beginning sufficient tax revenue to the states to prevent the 'natural' imbalance from arising. Such a solution immediately invites further questions on the suitability of various possible taxes for this purpose. The number of taxes which can be left entirely to the discretion of state governments is limited. Land and real estate taxes are one choice but there are limitations to these, as explained in Chapter 4; and local authorities also have strong claims on these. Excise taxes suffer from two drawbacks: first, there may only be a limited range of domestic products which can be taxed, and second, large differentials in rates of tax in different areas always lead to awkward frontier smuggling problems. The latter objection may not be very important if there are comparatively few unit governments and comparatively small differentials in tax rates but the same cannot be said of the former. Nor is the solution which is so favoured in North America – state sales taxes – of easy application in many underdeveloped countries, for the reasons elaborated at length in Chapter 3. There may be cases when export duties can be levied at the state level but if internal barriers to trade (or a complicated system of refunds) are to be avoided, this presupposes that direct contacts between any one state and the outside world are the normal practice – rather than exports passing through other

[1] The example given by Professor Newlyn, *Federalism and Economic Growth*, *op. cit.*, p. 101, of the effects of the rapid industrialisation of Kenya on the finances of Tanganyika (as it then was) and Uganda illustrates the problem nicely, even though there is no actual federal constitution in East Africa.

states on the way to ports. Such a state of affairs must be fairly rare, although the former West Indies Federation was a case in point. It is unthinkable that company taxation should be left entirely in the hands of individual states. Any such decision would lead to grave difficulties of apportionment of taxation in the case of companies straddling more than one state; furthermore, there would be no uniformity of tax rates payable by foreign firms and foreign capital and this might have serious disadvantages to foreigners contemplating investment in a country. Import duties will normally be a federal matter (except when there is no common tariff) and although personal income tax can be made a state responsibility as in Nigeria, it will not normally be possible for a federal government to waive all its rights to such an important tax.

If it proves impossible to bridge the financial gap of the states by making over rights to the total yield of various taxes, the next obvious solution is that of sharing tax yields with the federal government. There are several ways in which this can be done.[1] One is for the federal government and the state government to share the yield of a federally administered tax on some agreed basis. One possible basis is the amount of tax which is deemed to be collected from a particular state. Thus a major source of regional revenue in Nigeria in the 1950s was the allocation of a proportion of total import duties to the various regions on the basis of relative consumption of dutiable imported goods. In Canada, the provinces agreed during the Second World War that the federal government should rent the right to levy income and capital taxes; and in return pay back certain proportions of the amount collected from each province. This practice has now ceased but it is a good historical illustration of the 'principle of derivation', as it is often called.

Alternatively, the agreement between the federal and state governments may be on the basis of absolute amounts or percentages of a given tax yield without reference to the principle

---

[1] *Cf.* C. S. Shoup, *Public Finance, op. cit.,* Ch. 25, for systematic analysis.

of derivation. The agreement may only relate to the total amount distributable to the states or it may encompass the distribution to individual states. In the latter case, the basis of a state's tax share may be compensation for loss of pre-federation revenues (in the case of federation by aggregation) or, more likely, population or some other simple measure of need. In India, for instance, the federal government is bound to assign a certain percentage to the states as a whole, the further breakdown between states being partly on the basis of population and partly according to other criteria.

Yet another possibility is that instead of receiving an allocation from a purely federal tax, the states are allowed to add their own percentage tax rate on to the federal tax rate. The communes of Switzerland, for instance, levy a *centime additional* for every franc of cantonal income and capital taxes, the cantons and communes jointly assessing the tax and the communes collecting it. Similar sorts of arrangements were made between the former Western Region government of Nigeria and its local authorities.[1] The precise method of administration will clearly vary from country to country.

If taxation devices are insufficient to fill the gap between state revenues and expenditures, the other obvious solution is grants from the federal to the state governments. There are an infinite number of bases on which grants may be made, but perhaps the first distinction is between grants related to specific items of expenditure and those not so related. The former commonly takes the form of matching state expenditure on specific items, e.g. if the state agrees to spend £1 million on police services, the federal government may make a grant of a further £1 million to be earmarked for police services. The latter may be based on a number of indicators of needs such as population, numbers of children, mileage of road, and so on. The essential difference between a specific grant, which is paid for educational purposes, and a block grant, even if based on, say, numbers of schoolchildren, is that in one case the state will only get the grant if it does spend it on education, in the other there is no compulsion

---

[1] *Cf.* U. K. Hicks, *Development from Below, op. cit.*, p. 179.

to do so.[1] Finally, any type of grant may be fixed for a short period of time or more or less indefinitely.

We have seen that some of the main problems of federal finance stem from the passage of time; that even if one has perfect arrangements at the start of a federation, it is highly likely that they will go awry before long. There are, in principle, two ways of trying to meet such developments. One is to provide for a regular review of financial arrangements. Thus in India a Finance Commission has to be appointed every five years and its terms of reference are prescribed by the constitution. It must make recommendations about the share of union taxes to be paid to the states taken as a whole, the allocation of this sum among the states and the principles on which grants-in-aid should be made to the states. It was also strongly recommended by the 1958 Fiscal Commission in Nigeria that there should be a regular Fiscal Review Commission.[2] A second possible device is to try to arrange the tax and grant structure in such a way as to have self-corrective properties, so that if, for instance, a revenue-expenditure gap opens up in one constituent state of a federation, forces are quickly set in motion to offset it. Needless to say, this is exceedingly difficult to do, if only for the reason that there are so many possible ways in which any initial arrangements may come adrift. But the general sort of point which is relevant is that federal-state tax sharing arrangements ought to be on a percentage rather than a fixed sum basis. It is perfectly true that the first arrangement carries with it the risk that revenue yields may fall in a slump as well as the prospect that they will rise in a boom; and this may well have awkward short term consequences. But these are not likely to be as serious as the long term consequences of a fixed sum basis. Finally, it might be argued that another way of dealing with any federal-state imbalances which arise over the course of time is to set up an *ad hoc* fiscal review commission as and when needed. But the very absence of any

[1] A third type of grant, which may incorporate features of both of the others, is the *ad hoc* grant paid to states to tide over emergencies, natural disasters, etc. We shall not discuss this type further here.
[2] *Report of Fiscal Commission for Nigeria* (Cmnd. 481, HMSO, London, July 1958).

form of regular review is sufficient evidence that this solution is not wholly satisfactory.[1]

Possible Solutions

We have outlined some of the main problems of federal finance and the main methods employed to solve them historically. Can we now say anything in terms of general principles about the relative acceptability of these various methods? The first point of importance is the desired degree of political independence. If it is thought highly important to maintain the rights of the states *vis-à-vis* those of the federal government, one should favour as much financial autonomy of the states as possible. Tax revenues are superior to grants; and among tax revenues, one should prefer those which are entirely under the control of the states rather than those which are shared with the federal government. If grants have to be made, there will be a greater degree of autonomy for the states if they are unrelated to specific items of expenditure. The weight attached to these points will depend on the country and the tight or loose nature of the federation. But the general principles are clear enough.

The second main point is the basis of the distribution of grants or tax refunds between areas. Should one take the line that if one region is growing rapidly and another (with, say, the same population) is stagnating, then the right principle is to share out federal money on the basis of equal amounts per head in each region, or more per head in the first or more per head in the second? Distribution of tax revenues on a population basis would lead to the first solution. The derivation basis would in all probability[2] lead to the second and distribution according to 'need' would probably lead to the third. Our earlier discussion in this chapter brings out the complexity of these matters.[3]

[1] *Cf.* D. T. Lakdawala, 'The Four Finance Commissions of India', *loc. cit.*

[2] I.e. in all cases except when tax revenues are negatively correlated with income per head.

[3] *Cf.* R. A. Musgrave, 'A Fiscal Theory of Political Federalism', Universities-National Bureau, *Public Finances* (National Bureau of Economic Research, Princeton University Press, Princeton, 1961), for a discussion of this and related topics. The change in the Nigerian system after the 1958 Commission Report

A third point of principle is the extent to which government should interfere directly[1] with the allocation of resources. If a federal government offers grants to states which are tied to particular objects of expenditure – police, roads and so on – this is likely to push more resources into those 'industries' than would otherwise have been the case. (This is not *necessarily* so; even if grants are made to states on a lump-sum basis, they might choose to expand expenditure in the same direction. But the probability is that they would not do so.) Federal government interference can always be pleaded for on the grounds of social-private discrepancies, monopolistic competition and so on. But it is a moot point where justification on these grounds ends and where undue interference begins.

Finally, there is the question of the periodic adjustment and correction of initial arrangements. In principle, there are many advantages in a system which has automatic built-in correcting properties. But it is difficult to contrive and is not without its own disadvantages. It might well be argued, for instance, that it is inappropriate for state governments to be concerned with revenue surpluses in booms and deficits in slumps and that such anti-cyclical finance as there is should be a matter for the federal government alone. If an automatic system is ruled out, then it seems better to argue for a permanent body (e.g. the Australian, Grants Commission) rather than a specially appointed group, such as the Indian Finance Commission. There can be no question that the accumulated lore and wisdom of a permanent body, even though its individual members change frequently, is likely to be far greater than that of an organisation destined to regular births and deaths.

So much for the general principles of federal-state finances. There is one other topic to consider. We saw that one advantage of a federally administered area compared to a group of independent states is that it is likely to be able to raise external

(Cmnd. 481, *op. cit.*), from allocating import duties on a derivation basis to allocation (via a 'distributable pool') on the basis of population, general needs, etc, is an illustration of changing emphases over the years.

[1] Indirect interference can obviously come about as a result of policies primarily concerned with inter-area distribution of grants.

(and perhaps internal) loans more cheaply. It is important that there should be effective machinery to ensure that such opportunities are not wasted. This does call for some organisation which can co-ordinate borrowing by federal and state governments and ensure that the maximum advantage is taken of the better credit rating of federal governments. To go into details would be beyond our scope but there seems to be general agreement that one needs an organisation something akin to the Australian Loan Council, a joint federal-state body, which borrows on behalf of the States as well as the federal government. What one should avoid is any resemblance to the Canadian 'system' of allowing provinces more or less unrestricted borrowing facilities, in the American as well as in the domestic market.

Appendix:
The Finances of Small Countries[1]

I

In discussing this subject the first things to do are to specify the problem and to outline its general importance. Small countries can be defined in a variety of different ways but I shall concentrate here on small countries defined in terms of population as distinct from income or area. Obviously, the dividing line between small and large populations is arbitrary, but what I have in mind is something of the order of two and a half million people or so – roughly the size of a number of major urban areas in Western countries (e.g. Manchester, Birmingham, Boston). Naturally, the precise conclusions will differ if other arbitrary dividing lines are taken and this must be borne in mind throughout. Another point is the implicit assumption about the density of population per square mile. We might think in terms of countries having small populations but with an average density of population per square mile or a density which is less or greater than that found in the world at large. Our principal emphasis will in fact be on small countries with an average density of population, but we shall cast one or two glances at the more particular problems of those which are sparsely or densely populated as well.

One other point which will recur on a number of occasions should be made now. This is simply that if one is comparing small countries with larger ones, then one obviously has to watch for other reasons which might vitiate any comparisons. It is no good, for instance, comparing countries with small and large populations if they differ vastly in a variety of respects such as

[1] Reprinted from I. G. Stewart (ed.) *Economic Development and Structural Change* (Edinburgh University Press, 1969).

income per capita or geographical location in the world, or, for that matter, in the basic structure of their economic systems. By the latter, I mean simply that comparisons between small and big countries where the small one was run on more or less capitalist lines and the large one was run on Soviet-type lines would clearly not be very meaningful.

We now say something about the importance of this subject. In a sense, one need not look further than the UK in 1968 to justify this paper. With the movements for Home Rule or Independence in Scotland, Wales, etc, the problems we discuss in this paper obviously do concern us very closely in this country. However, to broaden the analysis, one can simply look at the *Unietd Nations Statistical Year-book*.[1] If one counts the number of countries for which population data are given, one finds that out of 139 independent countries, there are 37 with a population of less than $2\frac{1}{2}$ million; and out of 57 non-self-governing territories there are 52 with a population of less than $2\frac{1}{2}$ million. So if one adds these two groups together one has a total of 89 countries out of 196 with populations of less than $2\frac{1}{2}$ million. The reaction to such figures might be that countries cannot be simply enumerated one by one in this way, and that one must give greater weighting to countries which exercise large influence in the world, by virtue of their population, income, area, etc. However, it should be remembered that in the eyes of the United Nations, even if not those of the Lord, all animals are equal, and each independent country, at any rate, does have a single vote and no one country has more than that. We should also remember the talk about the pressure being exercised by the 77 developing countries at the second Unctad meeting in Delhi. Not all these 77 countries are in the small population class, of course, but nevertheless a substantial fraction is.

It might be argued that, even though there is a large number of small countries in the world today nevertheless it is likely to diminish rapidly in the future. I see no evidence whatever for a proposition of this sort, given the background of nationalistic feeling which one finds anywhere and everywhere in the world.

[1] *UN Statistical Yearbook* 1966 (New York, 1967).

Consider, for instance, how the number of countries might be reduced. First of all, there might be a voluntary merger, say, in the form of a federation. But the experience of federally united countries in recent years hardly gives one much reason for thinking that this development is going to be important in the near future. After all, the Federation of the West Indies and the Central African Federation both broke up in the early sixties; the union of Singapore and Malaysia was shortlived; the future of the East African Federation is by no means certain; and the Federation of Nigeria has tended to become looser over the years with the transition from three to four regions and, more recently, to twelve states. So it would not seem that this development is very likely. Alternatively, one might argue that the number of small countries would be reduced through a compulsory merger, i.e. through conquest or absorption. This could certainly happen but, once again, given the watching presence of international agencies and the like, one would have thought that this was a much less likely development than in the nineteenth century. So I should be surprised if this were to be an important phenomenon in the future. Thirdly, one might imagine that some countries could disappear simply by becoming uninhabited, say, in the way in which islands in the Outer Hebrides have become uninhabited during this century. Once again, one must judge this to be an unlikely development, given the pattern of world immigration laws.

I am therefore taking the view that we have a lot of small countries in the world today, and that we are likely to go on having a lot in the future. It is perfectly true that there have always been a number of small principalities, such as Monaco and Andorra in Europe, but some of the developments of the post-war world such as the breaking of colonial ties and the intense nationalistic fervour of many new countries make it likely that this phenomenon will be much more widespread in the future than it has been in the past.

It may be that after due exploration we shall find that the fact of smallness, as measured by population, is not a major issue for the finance of government either on the revenue or the expenditure side, but *prima facie* it seems a worthwhile exercise to inquire whether it is or not.

II

In this section I propose to look at some of the *a priori* arguments which might lead one to think that small countries would have a different financial set-up or a different set of financial issues to face compared to large countries. I do wish to emphasise that at this stage the argument is essentially that of the traditional armchair theorist, and we shall not become involved in any detailed empirical evidence until we reach the next section.

It may be useful, first of all, to try to deduce what some of the general economic characteristics of small countries are likely to be compared to large countries. Subsequently, we can consider in more detail the likely impact on the expenditure and revenue sides of government.

If we are to discourse on the general economic characteristics of small countries, one clearly has to specify some relevant alternative set of political arrangements. In this context, the comparison is often made between a small country and a big one notwithstanding the fact that the two are logically bound to differ from one another in respect of either land area or density of population – thereby tending to vitiate the comparison in one way[1] or another. It would seem more sensible to make a comparison between the characteristics of a number of small countries all independent of one another and, on the other hand, the characteristics of a united country embracing all the small ones. The precise form of the political organisation of the united country can reasonably be a matter of opinion, but perhaps it is most plausible to assume that it would be a loose kind of federation. This is, after all, the most likely alternative to having a series of independent states. The really important proposition is that for some purposes one wants to compare the characteristics of all the small countries taken together with those of the larger geographical area which forms the federation. It may be a reasonable simplification at some points to select one of the

[1] E.g. a greater land area is likely to mean greater opportunities for trade.

small countries (a 'representative country') to compare with the federal area, but the basic model must surely be that of comparing the whole congeries of small countries with the larger one. One could clearly think of other alternatives, e.g. a large area splitting up into a slightly less large one and another very small unit and then compare the characteristics of the two new units with the old one. But we shall not take that particular course of reasoning here.

Further clarification is also needed about the precise basis of comparison between the federated and the defederated positions. For some purposes, it will be sufficient to make the comparison on a simple before and after basis. But for other purposes we shall need to envisage how the economy might have developed over time if federation had continued relatively to the course of events in the various units after defederation.[1] We shall endeavour to make the precise basis of comparison clear in each case as we go along. The first point of comparison between the federated and the defederated positions is that, almost by definition, the volume of international trade relatively to internal trade will increase. Trade flows between the units which took place in the days of the federation were regarded as internal flows; now they must be regarded as international flows. So unless there is a very marked reduction in the amount of trade between the small units, taken all together, and the rest of the world, or unless there is a large reduction in the amount of trade flows between the units – or some combination of both these reductions – it must follow that the volume of international trade will increase. Another important consequence also follows defederation. Whereas a federation may well embrace a variety of different specialisations, this is far less likely for each individual unit. It follows from this that the likelihood of income fluctuation over time is much greater for the representative small country than for the federation as a whole.

[1] The advantage of assuming a federation initially, and then tracing the consequences of defederation rather than the other way round is that this is slightly more complex. One then has to think, for instance, about the disbanding of the federal government or the financial consequences if the former federal employees have to be absorbed in the new government structure.

The exact effects on the volume and pattern of international trade will obviously be dependent on the changes in tariffs and other protective devices (as well as any in relative costs, incomes, taxes etc) which come about as a result of the breaking up of the federation. There is no fundamental reason why a federation should be associated with free trade between the units (e.g. the West Indies Federation of the late 1950s); and there is no basic reason why trade between units which have defederated should be subject to protective devices of any kind. Nevertheless, it seems a reasonable assumption that the impediments to trade between the units are likely to be greater after the break-up of federation. There may also be upward changes in respect of tariffs, etc., between this group of countries and the rest of the world, for reasons we shall come to in a moment.

On the plausible assumption that impediments to trade between the units are likely to be greater once defederation has taken place, it would seem reasonable to hypothesise that the potentialities for the growth of manufacturing industry will be less than before. Purely on the grounds that the advantages of economies of scale are more likely to be fully reaped if one has a large domestic market than if one has to battle for external outlets, defederation will result in a larger volume of imported manufactures from the rest of the world and less domestic production than would otherwise have been the case.[1] The corollary is therefore that one may find a faster rate of growth of services, and perhaps of agriculture, and so on, after defederation, as the volume of employment in secondary activity will grow more slowly. To some extent, this proposition works in the opposite direction to that mentioned above, in that, if the volume of manufacturing production grows more slowly, there will tend to be less manufacturing trade flows between the units after defederation than would otherwise have been the case; unless this is compensated by larger flows of other products,

[1] Intensified policies of import substitution may prevent the absolute volume of output and/or employment in manufacturing from declining but it seems reasonable to assume that the rate of increase will nonetheless be smaller than it otherwise would have been.

there will therefore tend to be comparatively smaller trade flows *in toto* between the units. This, of course, does not controvert the general conclusion that the total amount of international trade will be greater after defederation than before.

There may be many influences other than tariff changes, affecting the volume of trade between the units. For instance, if defederation is accompanied by the growth or resuscitation of individual languages in the different units in substitution for some *lingua franca*, this might, in due course, lead to cultural differences and a reduction in the rate of increase of trade flows, quite apart from that due to any tariff barriers.

Given the general conclusion about a lower rate of growth of manufacturing industry in a situation of defederation, it is likely that the growth of the corporate sector of the economy will also be less, as this tends to be associated more with manufacturing than with other activities such as tourism, services or agriculture.

Another characteristic of defederated units is that one is then more likely to find a situation in which one or two firms are very powerful, relatively to the government. It could, of course, be the case that even in a federation a particular foreign firm, say, might play a part in every territory and therefore its overall size, relative, to that of the federal government, would be large. But it is much more likely that such foreign firms will be differentially important in the various units, and so the likelihood of their having positions of dominance is greater when one has a collection of small countries rather than a single federation. What I have in mind here is the dominance of particular firms such as the United Fruit Company in the banana republics of Central America. Quite apart from the general effects on the degree of competition, this will obviously have important repercussions on such matters as the government's bargaining power in respect of taxation, import or export prices, wages legislation and so on.

Another likely development is that the collectivity of small countries may be able to extract more in aid from Western countries than one federally organised area. It has become increasingly clear in recent years that aid does not increase proportionately to size of population, and so it would therefore follow that a number of small countries speaking with a number of different voices may be able to extract more *in toto* than would be the case with one single large organisation.[1] So even if the trade developments imply a reduction in the rate of increase of income per head, they may be partly or wholly compensated by increases in external aid. On the other hand, there are factors working for more inequality of income distribution between countries. There is no longer a federal government to reduce income disparities between units by suitable revenue or expenditure policies[2]; and in so far as movements of capital and labour are more likely to be inhibited by tax laws or other barriers if a number of countries defederate, inequality will be greater still. This would tend to be the case, for instance, even if restrictions on labour movements principally affected seasonal workers rather than long term permanent immigrants.

The precise result of these various changes on the growth of income per head in the defederated case is not easy to predict. If one thinks that the disadvantages of more impediments to trade, of a slower rate of industrialisation, and of the reduced rate of adoption of a corporate form of enterprise, etc, are important, one is likely to conclude that growth will be slower. But there are clearly many imponderables in reaching an exact conclusion and we do not pretend to reach one here. What would seem to be much clearer is that fluctuations of income over time will be greater, whatever the precise statistical technique of measuring them, as a result of greater specialisation among the independent units than would have been the case in the federation as a whole.

After this general review, we now look at the more specific characteristics of defederation which concern us here. First of

[1] *Cf.* I. M. D. Little and J. M. Clifford, *International Aid* (London, 1965), p. 94 for corroboration and also for reference to an unpublished econometric analysis by A. Strout.

[2] In so far as governments tend to concentrate expenditure (e.g. hospitals) on capital cities, defederation and an increase in relative importance of hitherto minor capitals might make for less rather than more inequality on the spending side.

all, what can be said about the government expenditure side? There are a number of points which immediately spring to mind. If one is contrasting a unitary government system for the whole area with a number of independent governments, the initial presumption is that one will have more in the way of government administrative expenses in the latter case. If, on the other hand, the comparison is between a federal system and independence the answer is not so clear, as one will in that case be eliminating one layer of government; though the savings in costs may be small if all the ex-federal employees have to be found new government jobs. Another general point is that there is likely to be greater contact and greater cohesion between the government and its population. This 'grass roots' argument could work in either of two directions. First, it is likely that pressures on governments to spend will be greater when the bulk of the population is just round the corner, so to speak. On the other hand, it can also be argued that with such a local government type of arrangement there is more likely to be willingness to pay on the part of the population for these expenditures. Which, on balance, of these two influences will predominate, it is impossible to say. The subject of economies of scale in government administration was explored by Professor Robinson at some length in a paper at an International Economics Association Conference[1] and I do not wish to add much to this here. He came to the general conclusion that although there are some obvious losses in small countries, especially small poor countries, e.g. the overheads of running a central bank or keeping foreign exchange reserves, or financing a university, or the maintenance of embassies and consulates abroad, there are also other economies such as the greater co-ordination and flexibility of government and so on. One particular point might be noted: in so far as there are potential losses due to the inability to employ their own specialists, small governments can by-pass such difficulties in much the same way as small firms can

---

[1] E. A. G. Robinson 'The Size of Nations and the Cost of Administration', E. A. G. Robinson (ed.), *The Economic Consequences of the Size of Nations* (London, 1960), Ch. 14.

by-pass the difficulties of not being able to have a large number of specialists on their payrolls. The standard procedure for small firms is to use a specialist agency. In just the same way small countries can belong to a common services organisation (e.g. East Africa) or have an associated states status, as in the West Indies; or they can call in international consultants to help them, say, appraise investment proposals involving government assistance; or they can join a defence alliance in order to economise on costs of military expenditures. Indeed, one can also argue that in so far as the ethnic cohesion of small countries is likely to be larger than that of large countries, this is, in turn, likely to mean less demands for policing than would otherwise be the case. One should not overdo this latter point in that saving in police might be offset by increases in expenditure on the armed forces, but it is simply an example of the sort of issue which arises. In his investigation, Professor Robinson looked into these matters of economies of scale in relation to administration, defence, economic services and social services, and came to the general conclusion that a small country (a 'representative small country' in our model) was not likely to be at any serious disadvantage. His argument was essentially that the number of devices available to avoid the diseconomies of small size is sufficiently large for this conclusion to hold over a wide range of country sizes ranging upwards from a relatively low level.

We now turn to the revenue characteristics which one may expect to find on *a priori* grounds in a representative small country. The first point is the ratio of total tax revenue to national income.

Are there any grounds for thinking that it may tend to be smaller or larger than in countries with larger populations? It is not easy to see any clearcut answer to this question. The grounds on which governments may intervene either in the sense of buying goods and services or in that of making larger amounts of transfer payments or in that of taking over the running of various sectors of the economy are multifarious, and there are no very strong reasons why one should find such a tremendous difference between small and large countries in this respect. One reason which may be important in some circumstances should be mentioned. The pressure on government to take over the running of public utilities and the like may be greater in a small country than in a large country where the availability of indigenous private enterprise for such purposes may be more likely. It seems a fair assumption to say that the likelihood of foreign companies or enterprises being allowed such concessions is fairly limited – unlike the nineteenth-century position – and so that possibility need not detain us too much. But this point apart, there are no obvious *a priori* reasons why one should expect the overall ratio to differ significantly between countries of different population sizes.

What does seem much more certain is that fluctuations in revenue will be greater from one year to another as a result of the greater fluctuations in GNP which we have already postulated. Although tax rates can be adjusted downwards when, say, incomes from exporting a particular crop rise, in practice adjustments may not be well-timed; and in the reverse case when incomes fall, it may be quite impracticable to raise tax rates sufficiently to stabilise revenues.

This brings us to the subject of direct taxes, whether on individuals or on corporations. There are several points which are relevant here. The first is that on the basis of our arguments about manufacturing industry and the corporate sector, one is likely to have a larger agricultural and services sector and a larger number of small firms or partnerships, sole traders, etc., than would otherwise have been the case. For these sorts of reasons then, one must be prepared to face the facts that company income taxes will yield less revenue and personal income tax may be relatively more diffiult to levy in the circumstances of small countries.

There are also some other points to note in respect of the operation of direct taxes. The first is that it is a well-known feature of many developing countries that they grant concessions to various enterprises which are often, though not necessarily, expatriate, in the form of tax holidays, accelerated

191

depreciation and so on. If one has a large number of small countries competing with one another in these respects, one is likely to find that the average degree of concession may well be greater than if the small countries were organised in the form of one single federal unit. Of course, this may not be so. If there are 90 countries in the world offering concessions, and the choice between federation and defederation only concerns two of them, one would not expect this to have much effect on the pattern of concessions. But it clearly remains a possibility. Whether it would have any substantial effect in reducing the amount of foreign investment is another issue requiring detailed analysis which would take us rather beyond the scope of our analysis here. The second point is that in a situation where one does have defederation on the lines envisaged, the chances are that a series of separate income tax systems will be introduced in these countries and over time they will begin to diverge in various minor, or even major, respects. Once this happens, the opportunities for tax avoidance and evasion tend to multiply. Companies locate their headquarter offices and arrange the organisation of their subsidiaries so as to minimise total tax outgoings; similarly, individuals, or at any rate those who are substantial taxpayers, will also arrange affairs to their own advantage. The old motto attributed to the residents on the borders between Northern and Southern Ireland ('Divided we stand; united we fall') has direct relevance here. Finally, it is worth observing that in the most successful federations – USA, Canada, Australia, for instance – there has been an increasing tendency over time for the central government to play a larger role in the assessment and collection of income tax. In Canada, for instance, the Dominion Government now collects personal income tax on behalf of all Provinces except Quebec and corporation tax on behalf of all except Quebec and Ontario – the two most populous, it might be noted. This experience does suggest that there are good reasons – political, as well as administrative and economic – for thinking that there are advantages in operating one large income tax system rather than a series of small ones.

What can be said about indirect taxes? The first observation is that if international trade flows are absolutely more important after defederation, this is likely to be a help rather than a hindrance in tax collection. Import and export taxes are customarily more easily levied than excise or sales taxes in developing countries.

On the other hand, foreign elasticities of supply to and demand for the products of any one small country will be greater than with a large one, and so the possibility of shifting the burden of such taxes to foreigners will be less. Furthermore, we have argued that a slower rate of growth of the manufacturing sector in the defederated case is likely to mean that agriculture will remain more important than it otherwise would have done. So fluctuations in tax revenues consequent on variations in agricultural output and/or prices will continue to be a major feature of tax systems.

We have made the point that government running of public utilities is virtually inevitable in small countries. There is a good deal of evidence to show that such operations usually tend to be a drain on general revenues rather than a support for them. So whatever the arguments for such operating losses in terms of economic efficiency of income distribution, we must expect them to add to budgetary strain.

A variety of other developments is likely. Although, as we saw above, the total amount of aid to the collectivity of small countries is likely to exceed that to the large one, the reverse is likely to be the case in respect of international borrowing terms. One would think, on *a priori* grounds, that the credit rating of a large country would be greater and so the terms of international borrowing less onerous.

One characteristic feature of many federal constitutions is the need to have regular fiscal reviews to share out revenues between the constituent countries. Although these reviews are settled amicably enough in some cases, in others they are the occasion for bitter and protracted bickering. At least this occasion for animosity would disappear if defederation took place. Finally, it may be worth observing that the EEC is proposing that most

193

of the taxes in the Community should in due course be harmonised. As the Community consists of a number of very different sized countries this suggests that the disadvantages of small size cannot be overwhelming for any tax; or that at least, if they are great for one tax, they are counterbalanced by opposing advantages for others.

III

At the risk of a charge of casual empiricism, we must confine ourselves to statistical evidence on a selected number of the points enumerated in our analysis. Moreover, our approach will often have to be an oblique one. It is also recognised that the statistical techniques used are very simple; more powerful ones could yield different answers.

We shall, in fact look at the position of small countries compared to a large one, under the following general headings, selecting particular points in each case:

1 Overall tax/GNP ratio
2 Government revenue composition
3 Government revenue collection efficiency
4 Government expenditure composition
5 Government expenditure efficiency

1. *Overall tax/GNP ratio*

There have been a number of attempts in recent years to explain overall tax/GNP ratios for different countries.[1] For our purposes the most useful is that by Lotz and Morss. Essentially, they tabulate the tax/GNP ratio for 52 developing countries, ranking countries according to the size of the ratio. Subsequently, using regressions, they standardise the tax/GNP ratio correcting,

---

[1] See e.g. A. M. Martin and W. A. Lewis, 'Patterns of Public Revenue and Expenditure', *The Manchester School*, September 1956; J. G. Williamson, 'Public Expenditure and Revenue: An International Comparison', *Manchester School*, January 1961; Harley H. Hinrichs, *A General Theory of Tax Structure Change During Economic Development* (Cambridge, Mass. 1966); R. S. Thorn, 'The Evolution of Public Finances during Economic Development', *Manchester School*, January 1967; J. R. Lotz and E. R. Morss, 'Measuring "Tax Effort" in Developing Countries', *IMF Staff Papers*, November 1967.

TABLE 1
Tax/GNP Ratios for 52 Countries

	Number of countries in:					
	High ratio bracket		Average ratio bracket		Low ratio bracket	
	Small	Large	Small	Large	Small	Large
Part A						
Tax/GNP ratio	0	12	6	17	2	15
Ratio adjusted for *per capita* income	1	11	3	20	4	13
Ratio adjusted for *per capita* income and openness	0	12	2	21	6	11
Part B						
Tax/GNP ratio	1	11	10	13	7	12
Ratio adjusted for *per capita* income	2	10	7	16	9	8
Ratio adjusted for *per capita* income and openness	4	8	4	19	10	7

Source: Lotz and Morss, *op. cit.*

Note: Total number in each high, average and low bracket is the same as that given in Table 4, Lotz and Morss, *op. cit.*

first, for differences in *per capita* income and, second, for differences in both *per capita* income and 'openness' (defined as the ratio of imports plus exports to GNP). The last ratio is considered to be a more reasonable indication of 'tax effort' on the grounds that one would expect tax/income ratios to differ between countries with differing *per capita* incomes or degrees of openness.

If one divides the 52 countries into large and small, one can then classify the Lotz and Morss findings as shown in Table 1.

(We start with a dividing line of $2\frac{1}{2}$m population in part A; but also try out another of 5m in part B, to see how sensitive the results are to any such change.)

There must clearly be many statistical reservations about any such results, e.g. the inevitable weakness of the data, and the unsatisfactory nature of some of these particular regression equations. But, for what they are worth, the results seem to show that after standardisation on both counts,[1] small countries are not able to achieve high tax/GNP ratios as easily as large ones, e.g. with the $2\frac{1}{2}$ million dividing line, 6 out of the 8 small countries are in the low bracket compared with only 11 of the 44 large; and with the 5 million dividing line 10 out of 18 small are in this category and only 7 out of 34 large. The differential effects of income per head and openness are such as to obscure this conclusion if one simply takes the crude tax/GNP ratios.

So it would appear that there is some evidence to show that relatively more small countries than large are likely to be in the low 'tax effort' category. This could be due either to a voluntary preference for relatively lower levels of public expenditure or to sheer inability to raise the same proportion of income in taxation. A study of the variations in revenue/expenditure ratios between countries might throw some light on this. But such an exercise must remain for the future.

2. *Government revenue composition*
We concluded earlier that one might expect small countries to raise a relatively larger proportion of their indirect taxes from import and export duties. The only data by which we can test this proposition are those in the *UN Statistical Yearbook*[2] and these may very well not fit the particular circumstances of our model. For what they are worth, we find that out of 26 developing countries, there are 11 with populations of less than 5m[3] and 15 with populations in excess. The unweighted mean ratio

---

[1] It would clearly be even better if the standardisation procedure could be carried further, e.g. by adjustment for differences and density of population.

[2] *UN Statistical Yearbook* 1966 (New York 1967).

[3] There were so few countries in the under $2\frac{1}{2}$ million class that any comparison would have been meaningless.

of import and export to total indirect taxes for the former is 60% and for the latter 58%. So on this basis, one clearly cannot conclude that there is any significant difference between small and large countries. However, all the reasons why the 11 may differ from the 15 in other respects (e.g. geography and history) must be remembered.[1]

3. *Government revenue collection efficiency*

Data are usually given in tax departments' reports about costs of collection. Such figures only refer to officially incurred costs; and international comparisons are likely to be hazardous. But, in one respect at least, there is a justification for making such comparisons. In so far as costs of collection are kept low at the expense of gathering less revenue, there will automatically be some degree of standardisation for quality of performance if we compare ratios of collection costs to revenue intake.

Examination of income tax department reports for a number of countries did not in fact suggest that variations in the collection/revenue ratio are clearly associated with size. One finds, for instance, that in three countries – Jamaica, Barbados, Mauritius – with similar systems inherited from British Colonial days – that the ratios were respectively 1%, 0.9% and 1.8% in recent years. Mauritius is smaller than Jamaica but has a higher ratio; Barbados is smaller than Jamaica but has a lower ratio. And, if it means anything to compare with the figure in an entirely different country, the UK, the 1965–6 figure there was 1.4. So it does not look as if one is going to find major differences between countries in pursuing this line of investigation.

Some miscellaneous evidence on this topic is to be found in Nigeria. In an investigation of income taxation in the old Western Region of Nigeria, Orewa[2] found that the larger the district the greater the degree of income tax evasion. For instance, in Ibadan district he estimated that in 1957–8 only 95,000 were

[1] It may be worth noting that of three countries with a measure of similarity in background, income levels, etc – India, Pakistan and Ceylon – the ratios were found to be 27%, 31% and 71% respectively. In this case there is a very clear difference between the smaller country and the larger ones.

[2] Oka Orewa, *Taxation in Western Nigeria* (Oxford 1962).

paying tax out of a possible 193,000; whereas in Iwo there were some 18,000 actual taxpayers out of a potential 19,000. Orewa attributed these very marked differences to the much greater personal contacts between first, tax rate assessors and collectors, and secondly, rate assessors and taxpayers in small communities. A further reason was that traders were more likely to be mobile and difficult to catch than rural workers; and the proportion of traders was likely to be greater in large urban areas. It must be remembered, however, that these findings relate to an income tax system with a substantial element of poll taxation in it.

More generally, Nigeria provides a good example of the problems of running a variety of income tax systems instead of a single one for the whole country.[1] Adedeji argued in 1965[2] that a single federal personal income tax system would have very considerable advantages over the five income tax systems then existing in terms of cheaper administration, more conformity of administrative practice, less evasion and so on. Given the more recent division of the country into twelve states, instead of four regions, this argument is surely overwhelmingly right, though the signs at the time of writing seem to point to the likelihood of at least 13 income tax systems in the country.

4. *Government expenditure composition*

It does not seem possible to deduce much from data on relative amounts spent under different heads. First, despite the very valuable work done by the UN in producing comparable data for a number of countries[3] the problems of non-uniform classifications are still formidable. Second, and more fundamental, even if we can ignore this point, it is difficult to see what conclusions can be drawn from simple comparisons of expenditure patterns in large and small countries. It may be that, say, the

[1] It could be argued that the case of Nigeria is contrary to what one would expect on the basis of our *a priori* conjectures in that one has a variety of income tax systems even within a federal structure. But it can be countered that a federal structure is a necessary, if not a sufficient, condition for avoiding such problems.

[2] A. Adedeji, 'The Future of Personal Income Taxation in Nigeria,' *Nigerian Journal of Economic and Social Studies*, July 1965.

[3] See e.g. *Statistical Yearbook* 1966, tables on public finances.

ratio of education to total expenditure is higher in a smaller country; this could be due to inescapable diseconomies of small size but it could also simply reflect relative income levels or relative preferences on the part of voters or their representatives. The ratio of defence to total expenditure is likely to depend on the hostility of neighbours or the possibilities of entering into alliances, just as much as, if not more than, on the size of population. Expenditure on roads is likely to be a function of density of population. Unless one can eliminate all these reasons for non-comparability, expenditure composition data will not be very illuminating.

5. *Government expenditure efficiency*

Inter-country comparisons of efficiency under different spending heads are useless unless allowances can somehow be made for such other variables as differences in quality of services provided. I know no means of doing this on an international basis. But comparisons between local authorities within a given country may shed some light, even if very obliquely, on the problem.

In the UK, there are various sources from which we can build up some impressions – in this context, a more appropriate word than conclusions. A few years ago the Royal Commission on Local Government in Greater London came to the conclusion that there was no optimum size of local authority in economic terms.[1] The Rural District Councils Associations recently gave evidence to the Royal Commission on Local Government in England and Wales.[2] Chapter 6 of this document made an analysis of costs of administration incurred by local authorities in providing a standard list of services. Although there was a small tendency for costs per head of population to fall with the size of the authority (e.g., for small county boroughs the figure was about £1.7 per head; for large ones it was £1.6) the general conclusion was that there were no important diseconomies of small size within the ranges covered (roughly, 30,000–400,000 population). The pertinent point was made that reorganisation

[1] *Report*, Cmnd. 1164 (HMSO, October 1960) p. 72.
[2] *Evidence of Rural District Councils Association*, 1966.

of functions, boundaries, etc., is a much more likely cause of cost increases than the small size of authorities.[1]

Detailed figures are published each year by the Institution of Municipal Treasurers and Accountants for local authority expenditure in England and Wales. As an experiment, the data on police expenditure for the different county boroughs[2] were analysed. A rough correction for quality of service was made by comparing groups of towns for which there was a very similar ratio of population to policemen. Given this element of standardisation, it was then possible to compare police expenditure per head of population between towns. The result was that there was no systematic variation with size and no evidence to suggest that small authorities, at any rate within the range covered (minimum size 65,000) suffered relatively to larger ones. Too much should not be read into these figures: the standardisation was very crude (e.g., crime rates may differ considerably between towns even if they have the same number of policemen per thousand population), the statistical techniques used were rough and ready and immediate application to countries with entirely different backgrounds, levels of income and so on would be foolhardy. The experiment was simply a very crude one which needs to be repeated on a much larger scale and refined pattern.

As another example of intracountry comparisons of expenditure efficiency, we may take Kiesling's investigation into education expenditure in New York State.[3] In a multiple regression analysis of educational performance with respect to pupil intelligence, school district, size, etc, in 97 school districts, he was not able to find any evidence of economies of scale with respect to size, as measured by average daily attendance at all schools in the district. If anything there was a hint of diseconomies of scale.

It may be worth remarking that in countries as different as the UK and Australia, grants from the central government to lower

[1] This point is very relevant to the situation of Nigeria in 1968, with the prospect of 13 major administrations (federal government plus 12 states) instead of 5.

[2] Institute of Municipal Treasurers and Accountants, *Police Force Statistics* 1966–7 (London, January 1968).

[3] H. J. Kiesling, 'Measuring a Local Government Service; a Study of School Districts in New York State', *Review of Economics and Statistics*, August 1967.

tiers have for many years given extra weight to those areas with low population densities, on the grounds that they had special burdens to bear in respect of such items as road maintenance, school upkeep, etc. So even though there is not much evidence of differences in expenditure performance between a representative small population and a large one,[1] there are grounds for distinguishing those small sized units which are lightly populated.

But it must be strongly stressed that conclusions drawn from local authorities in relatively advanced countries cannot be applied across the board to the much less developed countries we have in mind in this paper. Such conclusions are no more than a start to any proper statistical investigation.

How can we summarise these very scattered and very variegated pieces of empirical evidence? There is some evidence to show that small countries make smaller 'tax efforts' than large ones, once allowances have been made for differences in income per head and in openness of the economy. But it is difficult to say exactly what interpretation should be placed on this result. As far as government revenue goes, there does not seem to be much in the proposition that small countries are likely to raise a larger fraction of their indirect taxes from import and export duties; but possibly rather more in the fear that a multiple system of income taxes leads to difficulties. On the expenditure side, comparisons of relative amounts spent under different headings are not likely to be very meaningful; and such evidence as there is on expenditure efficiency does not suggest that small countries necessarily suffer in this respect.

A great deal more work needs to be done before any conclusions can be advanced with any confidence of any sort. But at this stage the very tentative impression must be that whatever the larger political and economic consequences of defederation (or of any alternative political machinery by which small countries are created) there is no overwhelming evidence of disastrous results necessarily following in the public finance field.

[1] It might be noted the UK formulae for central government grants to local authorities have never had any components based on economies of scale.

Selected References

A. Adedeji, *Nigerian Federal Finance: its Development, Problems and Prospects* (Hutchinson, London, 1969)

R. Bird, *Bibliography on Taxation in Developing Countries* (Harvard Law School, Cambridge, Mass., 1968)

R. Bird, *Public Finance and Economic Development* (Harvard University Press, Cambridge, Mass., 1970)

R. Bird and O. Oldman, *Readings on Taxation in Developing Countries* (Johns Hopkins, Baltimore, 1967)

R. J. Chelliah, *Fiscal Policy in Underdeveloped Countries* (second edition, Allen and Unwin, London, 1969)

J. F. Due, *Taxation & Economic Development in Tropical Africa* (M.I.T. Press, Cambridge, Mass., 1963)

J. F. Due, *Indirect Taxation in Developing Economies* (Johns Hopkins, Baltimore, 1970)

C. T. Edwards, *Public Finances in Malaya and Singapore* (Australian National University Press, Canberra, 1970)

J. Heller and K. Kauffman, *Tax Incentives in Less Developed Countries* (Harvard Law School, International Program on Taxation, Cambridge, Mass., 1963)

U. K. Hicks, *Development from Below* (Oxford University Press, Oxford, 1961)

U. K. Hicks, *Development Finance* (Oxford University Press, Oxford, 1965)

N. Kaldor, *Indian Tax Reform* (Ministry of Finance, Delhi, 1956)

R. A. Musgrave, *Fiscal Systems* (Yale University Press, New Haven, 1969)

Organisation of American States (Joint Tax Program), *Fiscal Policy for Economic Growth in Latin America* (Johns Hopkins, Baltimore, 1965)

Organisation of American States (Joint Tax Program), *Problems of Tax Administration in Latin America* (Johns Hopkins, Baltimore, 1965)

A. T. Peacock and G. Hanser (eds), *Government Finance and Economic Development* (OECD, Paris, 1965)

A. R. Prest, *A Fiscal Survey of the British Caribbean* (HMSO) London, 1957)

C. S. Shoup *et al.*, *The Tax System of Liberia* (Columbia University Press, New York, 1970)

C. S. Shoup *et al.*, *The Fiscal System of Venezuela* (Johns Hopkins, Baltimore, 1959)

M. C. Taylor, *Taxation for African Development* (Hutchinson, London, 1970)

H. P. Wald, *Taxation of Agricultural Land in Underdeveloped Countries* (Harvard University Press, Cambridge, Mass., 1959)

Note: This list is confined to books specialising on public finance in developing countries.

Index

205

Fiji, 34
Fiscal Methods, importance of, 29–31
Forward estimates, 150–2
Friedmann, J., 164n
Furtado, C., 89

Galletti, R., 69n
Gantt, A. H., 11, 30n, 127n
Ghana, 26
Gittes, E. F., 157n
Glassburner, B., 125n
Goode, R., 66n, 68n
Greece, 134
Griffin, K. B., 125n
Guinea, 102

Hailey, Lord, 91n, 142
Hansen, B., 110n, 153n
Hart, A. G., 41n, 47n, 78n, 105, 112, 141n, 143n
Hauser, G., 110n, 203
Head, J., 12n
Healey, J. M., 101
Helleiner, G. K., 71n, 72n
Heller, J., 202
Hicks, J. R., 84n
Hicks, U.K., 14n, 84n, 126n, 147n, 161n, 168n, 176n, 202
Higgins, B., 143
Hinrichs, H. H., 194n
Hirao, T., 141n
Hirschman, A. O., 92n, 167n
Huiskamy, J. C. L., 42n

Import duties, 63–6
Income, definition of, 34–5
Income, measurement of, 35–8; see also: subsistence
Income tax, children's allowances, 43–7; collection of, 41–2; effects of, 39–40; rates of, 38–9; role of, 33; see also: company taxation
India, 19, 77, 82, 86n, 170
Indonesia, 130
Inflation, and tax revenue, 141–2
Investment concessions, 51–3, 55–8; Nigeria, 59

Jain, M. M., 28n
Jamaica, 34, 46, 197
Jetha, N., 48n

Kaldor, N., 79n, 143, 163, 202
Kauffman, K., 202
Kennedy, C., 97n
Keynes, Lord, 86n
Khalid, R. O., 156n
Kiesling, H. J., 200n
King, T., 167n

Lakdawala, D. T., 170n, 178n
Land taxation, arguments for, 80–90; new ideas, 92–4; problems of, 90–2
Land value increments, taxation of, 94–9
Layard, P. R. G., 123n, 126n
Lefeber, L., 167n
Lent, G. E., 56n, 58n, 66n, 68n, 75n, 81n, 90, 97n, 98n, 102n
Lewis, Sir W. A., 38n, 124n, 135n, 194n
Liberia, 39, 65, 74
Little, I. M. D., 59n, 101n, 188n
Lloyd, George D., 158n
Lotz, J. R., 20n, 194n
Lovasy, G., 154n

MacBean, A. I., 10n
McCawley, P., 130n
McCrone, G., 160n
Maddison, A., 14n
Malaysia, 20n, 27, 34n, 60, 67, 78, 120n, 154
Marketing Boards, 70–3
Martin, A. M., 38n, 194n
Mauritius, 10, 26, 46, 56, 197
Meade, J. E., 10, 46, 56, 59n, 116n
Mexico, 33
Mill, J. S., 95
Mishan, E. J., 103
Morley, Lord, 9
Morss, E. R., 20n, 194n
Musgrave, R. A., 13n, 20, 21n, 24n, 137n, 167n, 178n, 202

DATE DUE

JAN 22 '79			